THE EMERGING WARRIOR BRIDE

A PROPHETIC REVELATION OF
THE BRIDAL PARADIGM

BY JUDITH VALENCIA

Unless otherwise indicated, all Scripture quotations are taken from the *King James Version* of the Bible.

Scripture quotations marked NKJV are from the New King James Version®. Copyright © 1982 by Thomas Nelson. Used by permission. All rights reserved.

Scripture quotations marked TPT are from The Passion Translation®. Copyright © 2017, 2018 by Passion & Fire Ministries, Inc. Used by permission. All rights reserved. ThePassionTranslation.com.

Scripture quotations marked (NIV) are taken from the Holy Bible, New International Version®, NIV®. Copyright © 1973, 1978, 1984, 2011 by Biblica, Inc.™ Used by permission of Zondervan. All rights reserved worldwide. www.zondervan.comThe "NIV" and "New International Version" are trademarks registered in the United States Patent and Trademark Office by Biblica, Inc.™

Scriptures marked NAS are taken from the NEW AMERICAN STANDARD (NAS): Scripture taken from the NEW AMERICAN STANDARD BIBLE®, copyright© 1960, 1962, 1963, 1968, 1971, 1972, 1973, 1975, 1977, 1995 by The Lockman Foundation. Used by permission.

The Emerging Warrior Bride: A Prophetic Revelation of the Bridal Paragdigm

ISBN 978-0-9910098-5-5

Copyright © 2020 Judith Valencia
Website: MyMorningWalksWithGod.com

Published by Inspired Design & Graphics

Printed in the United States of America. All rights reserved under International Copyright Law. Contents and/or cover may not be reproduced in whole or in part in any form without the express written consent of the Publisher.

TABLE OF CONTENTS

Foreword 5

A Revelation of God's Love 9

Let Him Kiss Me.. 33

I Am Dark But Lovely 55

Finding Your Place at the King's Table 79

Winter is Past!.. 101

Your Face is Lovely... 121

Withdrawn Presence.. 141

The Royal Wedding... 161

The Jewish Wedding Ceremony...................... 183

Closing Remarks 211

FOREWORD

This is the most amazing time to be alive. The book you are holding, *The Emerging Warrior Bride*, will bring you into a deeper relationship with Christ. It will help God's people navigate to their creative destiny of love and intimacy with their King. This is a NOW book!

I have known Apostle Judi Valencia for over ten years. When we met, she was teaching at a Bible School that I was attending. Immediately, I realized she was someone I wanted to be around. Besides her profound and timely teachings; her intimacy, love and devotion to our Lord was beautiful to watch.

I watched her pour out love as she taught her women's group. During those meetings I witnessed a group of women who had a high regard for her. They gleaned from her teachings as they received honor and honored each other. Not to mention those meetings were run like a 'fine oiled machine'.

Many people could see that she was and is a true Apostle. Most people focus on the aspect of being an apostle as a 'sent' one. That is true. But, the equally important aspect is one who is in an intimate relationship with their King. This is evident in Judi's life.

During my prayer time one afternoon, I saw a vision of Judi going into her house, and entering her room and closing the door.

The Lord was showing me a person who "dwells in the secret place of the Most High God". As we began to spend time together, it was very apparent we both wanted one thing and one thing alone. A deeper and intimate relationship with Christ.

When I heard Apostle Judi's teaching on the Bridal Paradigm my life changed. It changed for a number of reasons. I have read the Song of Solomon for years. I truly searched for the deeper meaning of that book. I have always believed it represented God's love toward us. There is certainly much depth in that book, but I did not discover it until I heard Judi's teaching.

That same day I asked Judi to come to my women's group to teach about this amazing love story found in what is called "The Song of All Songs". It was a glorious occasion.

Apostle Judi brings forth the love Christ has for us His bride, like no other teacher or preacher that I have heard. In order for us to truly understand who we are in Christ, we must first encounter His deep, astounding love for us. Then and only then, can we take part in the Paradigm shift so desperately needed in this hour we are in. She is able to do that through this love story.

This is a deep teaching, as Judi takes it line by line in some places. She explains how Christ glances at us and speaks to us. Explaining His every move toward us in His pursuit of us! WOW!! Once we get that, we know we are part of this Bridal Paradigm. You see, Judi penned the term 'Bridal Wave'. It will show us how to live as His bride, function as His family, and move in and own His Authority!!

She explains that the Paradigm shift in the body of Christ is about thinking and living like His Bride. His end-time bride!! She explains that we are Mrs. Jesus Christ! Chew on that for a while (as you finish the book, of course).

Judi also overcomes any uncomfortable moment or thought that men might have when they hear they are also Christ's Bride. *The Emerging Warrior Bride* is absolutely for both men and women. Remember what Paul said, "there is neither male or female in the Kingdom".

One last point about *The Emerging Warrior Bride* and why you need to read this book and live in this shift - Judi makes the connection that the Song of Songs is connected to the book of Revelation. She explains how these two books are our two most important 'end time' books of the Bible. They go together. Well, she hit that one out of the park!!

Now more than ever we need to make sense of the end times we are in. She states that we are going to a wedding feast. Christ is coming back for a healthy Bride, not a sick religious church. This book will bring down the religious church structure currently running rampant on the earth!!

The Emerging Warrior Bride will completely change your life!! The deepest love explained the deepest way!!

Laurie Rahter
Face to Face Int'l. Ministries
Prophetic Teacher, Minister And Revivalist

CHAPTER 1
A REVELATION OF GOD'S LOVE

Some of us have struggled for years to understand and know the love of God. One of the main reasons for this is because there are blockages that have come into our lives from our past, from our upbringing, and just from living in this fallen world. God wants to bypass all of those blockages and go right to our hearts, to show us the depth of His great love.

Comprehending the love of God is something that is easier *caught* than *taught*. You see, I can tell you that you are loved. I can tell you who you are in Christ. I can teach you how much He loves you. But, His love for you goes beyond my limited comprehension and ability to teach about it. So, ultimately, you have to receive it by way of revelation. The eyes of your understanding have to be opened for your spirit man to truly "get it." That's what I pray over you as you receive this teaching of The Bridal Paradigm. I pray that you receive a new revelation of God's love for you, and that you will *"know the love of Christ that surpasses knowledge, that you may be filled with all the fullness of God"* (Ephesians 3:19).

We are going to be the end-time bride of Christ… the glorious end-time Bride… not the religious, defeated, dead, dry, end-time

Bride. As His Bride, we want to be a reflection of our Bridegroom, and of our King. It is a beautiful thing. I want men to understand that this teaching is for them, as well as for women. So, men, just buckle your seat belts… before this ride is over, you will come to understand that you, too, are the Bride of Christ.

WHAT IS A PARADIGM?

Why have I entitled this book "The Bridal Paradigm?" What does *paradigm* mean, anyway? The word paradigm means "an example, or a pattern, or a model of something." So what I'm going to be sharing with you is an illustration, or a pattern of what the Bride of Christ is supposed to look like in these last days.

The first time I taught this message was to a women's Bible study group. There were about fifty to seventy-five women in the group. We had a big, fat syllabus that I taught from, and it took me every bit of nine months to teach it. Now, this teaching is based off of the Song of Solomon, which is only eight chapters long. So, you might ask, "How can a book of only eight chapters take so long to teach?" It's because once you get into this book, you begin to understand that it's more than just a book of songs written by Solomon. You discover that it is actually one of two end-time prophetic books that God gave to the Church.

A PROPHETIC BOOK

That's right! Song of Solomon is an end-time prophetic book. You probably already know that the book of Revelation is the other end-time prophetic book. Song of Solomon is often called *The Song of All Songs*. That's because Solomon wrote one thousand and five songs, but this one was the very best. It truly is *The Song of All Songs*, because it is the love song of the Bridegroom to his Bride.

So, both Revelation and Song of Solomon are prophetic. If you tried to take every passage in these two books literally, they might not make sense, because there is a deeper meaning than what is seen on the surface. We need the Spirit of God to help us understand the meaning in these books because of their prophetic nature.

It's also important to understand that these two books go hand-in-hand. Many people study the book of Revelation and try to teach it to the church today, but without the revelation found in Song of Solomon concerning the Bride. The book of Revelation tells us that things are being prepared for a banquet… for a *marriage supper* (Revelation 19:9). It also tells us that "His bride has made herself ready" (Revelation 19:7). These references in Revelation point back to the bride in Song of Solomon.

HE'S COMING BACK FOR A BRIDE

The Church today is not living in its proper dispensation. She's still functioning as the Church of yesterday, instead of becoming the end-time Bride in the dispensation we're in now. Please hear that! A lot of our mindsets, and traditions, and church mentality are boxed into what *was*… what we've been *in the past*. But God is wanting us to become the Bride. If you hear nothing else I say, hear this. He's not coming back for a *Church*… He's coming back for a *Bride*! It's time for the Church to start acting like a Bride!

It's time for the Church to start loving like a Bride… like a Bride preparing herself for her wedding day. Yes, we need to start thinking like a Bride.

The Song of Solomon is a book that many in the Body of Christ avoid. Let's be honest about it. If you've been reading through the Bible and then come to Song of Solomon it's like "Ugh, O' Lord!" Am I right? There are understandable reasons for that response and I will be addressing those reasons.

But, the Song of Solomon is a teaching about God's heart for His Bride, and it's a teaching about the *love affair* God wants to have with His Bride. Perhaps you're thinking, "Judi, you're getting a little too intimate." Listen, I don't know one bridegroom that doesn't want to be intimate with his bride. Hello! But, it seems like the Church of today is afraid of intimacy. Slowly say that word "intimacy" and you discover why people are afraid of it… "in-to-me-see." Ah! That's the problem! We don't want God to get so close to us that He can "*see in to me.*" We'd rather Him stay at a safe distance… close enough to help us if we have a problem, but not so close that He can see into the inner recesses of our heart. Here's a news flash for you… He already knows what's in there, yet that hasn't stopped His love from reaching out to you. As a matter of fact, it accelerated His love all the way to the cross.

This teaching can, and will, transform your life with Jesus. It's what every heart longs for. Every single person on this planet has something within their spirit man that God put there, and it says, "*Somebody love me. Somebody love me for who I am. I don't have to be somebody I'm not. I don't have to pretend. I don't have to put on airs. I can just be me, and that's enough.*"

Every single human being on this planet wants and longs for the love of God, whether they realize that's what they're longing for or not. I'm not just talking to women, here. This is not a teaching for women only, for in Christ, "*there is neither male nor female*" (Galatians 3:28). We are all the *Body* of Christ, which means we are all the *Bride* of Christ.

THE DIFFERENCE BETWEEN MEN AND WOMEN

Teaching this to women is less challenging than teaching it to men. The first time I brought this message to both men and women together, the men in the room said, "Don't make me a Bride… don't put a veil on my head… No!" They didn't want to be feminized. They didn't understand or appreciate what it means to be a bride. So, teaching this to men has definitely been a challenge, and God has shown me ways to present it to men so they can receive it better. But women know what it's like to be a bride, even if they've never been married before. It's just *in* a woman. God put that inside them… that desire to be a beautiful bride. God gave us this example, this visual. The world didn't put this desire in women. God did! God wants women to *want* to be a Bride.

Men, on the other hand, are pursuers by nature. The bride (the woman) is the one being pursued. By nature, women know what it's like to be pursued. So, if you tell a woman that Jesus is pursuing her, that He loves her and He wants her to be His Bride, it's easy for her to understand. However, if you tell a man, "Jesus loves you and He's pursuing you, and He wants to make you His Bride," something in the male brain short circuits. That's because men and women are wired differently. Women have an emotional side of their brain that they see the world through, whereas men have a more logical, practical side. So, I'll have to present this in a more practical, logical way to reach the men who are reading this.

As I said before, men are pursuers. So if a man wants to know how to relate to the bridal paradigm, he must first understand that God is a pursuer, too. A man knows what it's like to be a pursuer. He knows what it's like to see something or someone that he wants so badly that he's willing to sell out completely and go after it all the way… to give it his all. Well, that's the way God is pursuing you, men. He wants you to be His. He's pursuing you in the same way you've pursued the things you've desired in your life.

Men like the idea of Jesus being their Hero, or being a mighty warrior. It's a lot easier for men to relate to Jesus in this way, or even as their buddy or best friend. It's a lot more difficult for a man to think of Jesus as their lover, or as their spouse. The macho side of men prevents them from thinking in that way. Women, however, have no problem in thinking of Jesus in that way. Women want a knight in shining armor to come and rescue them. Men would rather *be* the knight in shining armor. They'd rather be the rescuer. Well, Jesus is both! He's our hero and warrior, but He's also our King, coming on His white horse to deliver us and rescue us. He's coming to sweep us off our feet so we can ride off with Him into the sunset together. Both of these are found in Jesus… something that men can relate to, and something women can relate to.

Now, I've already mentioned that there are two end-time prophetic books in the Bible, and that's Song of Solomon and Revelation. In the book of Revelation, you'll see several inferences to the fact that Jesus is returning for a Bride. Ephesians gives more detail about this Bride: "*That He might present her* [His Bride] *to Himself a glorious church, not having spot, or wrinkle or any such thing; but that she should be holy and without blemish*" (Ephesians 5:27). We are that end-time Bride. You know this in your head, but I'm praying that you will receive revelation of this in your heart, and that it becomes a part of you… that you will actually take on that role and that position as the Bride of Christ. Again, this message is not for "*the Church*"… it's for "*the Bride.*"

So, first, we must learn that we are the Bride, and then we must walk more confidently in who we are as that Bride. There have been prophetic utterances that speak of an end-time revival that will be a tidal wave in the Spirit realm. But, I truly believe God told me that this end-time revival will be a *Bridal Wave*. Did you hear that? It will be a Bridal Wave of His glory. There's going to be a wave of glory that's going to hit the Church and reveal the Bride in this hour. The glorious Bride who is passionately in love with her King!

THREE THINGS MUST HAPPEN

I'm going to lay a foundation for this teaching before we delve into it. Three things must happen before we begin.

Number One: We must realize that God is Spirit.

Yes, we call God *Father* and we call Jesus *Son*, but in Christ there is neither male nor female. There is no sex label or gender label in the Spirit realm. That's been one of the stumbling blocks for the Church when we read Song of Solomon because we're thinking in terms of this world: male and female. We're thinking on a sexual level instead of a spiritual level, so we're not capturing the true essence of the book.

In the Song of Solomon, we'll be reading about how a king pursues a peasant Shulamite woman who has been working in the vineyard. Her brothers have put her in the vineyard. She doesn't want to be there. She's gotten sunburned and tanned (which represents sin). She says, "Don't look at me, because I'm dark. I'm stained." She sees this gorgeous, glorious, beautiful, perfect king who's pursuing her and all she sees is her filth. All she sees is how dirty and stained she is. And, she says, "My brothers were angry at me and they made me work in this vineyard."

A BANNER CALLED "LOVE"

Have you ever been forced to do something you didn't want to do? It hurt you. It stained you. This Shulamite woman was being put in a situation that she didn't want to be in. On top of that, she was having to neglect her own vineyard because her brothers were making her work in theirs. So, she's angry because she's being forced into this situation, but she's also feeling neglected. Have you ever felt like that? Can you relate? This book is going to take you on a journey where the king brings this stained, neglected Shulamite woman into his chambers and puts a banner over her called *love*. If you're born again, you have that very same banner over you. This world can say every bad thing about you that they want to, but God has placed His banner over you. In ancient times, when soldiers went into battle, they'd raise a banner over their army. And, when they returned home in victory from their battles, they'd wave that banner in celebration. When Christ won the battle against Death, Hell and the Grave, He said, "The banner that I am now waving over you is *love*." Those old banners of hate, sin, and rejection are no longer over your life! You have a new banner over you. It was put there by your victorious Lord. That banner is called *love*!

There are parts of the story in Song of Solomon where the king removes himself from her. She says, "I'm hiding behind the lattice. He can't find me." There are many things each of us hide behind, just like this Shulamite woman did. We hide because we don't want God to get too close. So, when she pulls herself away and hides from the king, he removes himself. How many times has God removed His presence from you so that you'll pull closer to Him? Unfortunately, we don't see those moments correctly. We see them as, "Oh, God's gone away. He's rejected me." No! He's saying, "Come closer. Come away with me." He's wooing you to come closer to Him during those times.

There are so many different things going on in the relationship between the king and the Shulamite woman in the Song of Solomon, and it's very symbolic of the relationship between the Lord and His Church. But, the end part of chapter 7 and beginning of chapter 8 is going to take you to a whole new place in your walk with the Lord. We're going from the place in chapter 1 where we see this poor, stained, neglected Shulamite peasant woman, to the place where we see a transformed woman in chapter 8, where it says, "Who is this coming up out of the wilderness?" (Song of Solomon 8:5). Who is this person? She's not the same woman she used to be. The Church of Jesus Christ has been in a wilderness for a very long time, and the world has not seen the Bride rise up yet. But the world is about to see this glorious, transformed Church rise up out of the wilderness as the Bride of Christ and it will startle them. They'll say, "Who is this? I've never seen this before!" They're coming up out of the wilderness… (and here's the key to the whole thing) "They're leaning on their beloved" (Song of Solomon 8:5). The two are arm-and-arm. They're shoulder-to-shoulder, walking side-by-side. She's not by herself anymore, *playing* church, trying to *be* the Church. She's now walking side by side with her husband. Husband and wife are united. Bride and Bridegroom are now in ministry together.

IT'S NOT A SEX MANUAL

When we read chapter 8, we find out that they're going into the vineyards together. When we read about her breasts in chapter 7 and 8, we all get embarrassed and uncomfortable. We say, "Oh no! The Bible is getting too risqué." Again, we've been reading it in a sexual context, but we have to remember that this is a spiritual thing. With her breasts, she's feeding the nations. She's now caring for others. She's nursing the new born babes in God's Kingdom who need the *"sincere milk of the Word"* (1 Peter 2:2). The end-time Bride of Christ is fruitful, nurturing and reproducing.

So, you're going to learn how to not look at this as a male-female thing, but to look at it in the Spirit realm, as God referring to His end-time Bride. Do not read this book as a sex manual. Read it as a love story from your King Jesus to His end-time Bride that He is passionately in love with. We are that Bride. Every one of us who are in Christ, whether we are male or female... because, *"there is neither male nor female: for ye are all one in Christ Jesus"* (Galatians 3:28).

Number Two: This is a Prophetic Book

Because this is a prophetic book, we are not going to look at it in an analytical sense. Many who love the Lord avoid reading this book because they don't have the proper mindset when they read it. It makes them uncomfortable. Men get uncomfortable reading, *"Let him kiss me with the kisses of his mouth"* (Song of Solomon 1:2) because they envision another man kissing them on the lips. Instead, they should be seeing a king who died for them, who loves them, kissing their spirit with His words, with His love that changes everything.

Many women become uncomfortable because Jesus is now becoming their *lover*. To some women this is a very difficult concept to grasp, because they've come out of a very religious background and mindset. We can't become the Bride if we have a religious mindset. Many have no problem calling Jesus their Lord, their Savior, their Master or even their best friend. But Jesus wants to become even more than that… He wants to become our lover and husband. And, He wants them to become His passionate Bride. This sounds almost sacrilegious to the religious mindset. Yes, many will say, "Hold on just a second! Jesus is Lord and Savior and I'm comfortable with that." But, Jesus isn't coming back for a comfortable Church. He's coming back for a passionate Bride!

So, again, this book is not a sex manual. I'm not saying that it won't help your marriage if you read it. I'm just saying that we've got to remember that this is a prophetic book, and it should be read as such.

Number Three: This Book is a Love Story

This book is a love letter to the Bride of Christ from her King. Now, the reason we interpret it incorrectly, and I must say this as delicately as possible, is because the world has perverted the definition of marriage for decades upon decades. It's to the point now where marriage is barely recognizable in comparison to the institution God originally ordained and created in the Garden of Eden between one man and one woman. God ordained marriage to be a holy union. He gave it to us as a visual. He gave it as a representation of the union between the Body of Christ and His beloved Son. When the man and the woman are married *"two become one."* They are no longer separate individuals. God is saying, through the marriage union, "I want to be married to you, and I want the two of us to become One."

MARRIAGE IS UNDER ATTACK

But Satan, on purpose, has perverted the meaning of marriage. He has perverted even the purity and sanctity of the marriage bed, where it is no longer holy, and only between a man and a woman. Just read today's headlines in the newspaper and you can see the dramatic change that has taken place in our society. Yes, this has been done on purpose, to pervert people's minds, to prevent them from seeing the connection between earthly marriage and the heavenly marriage of Christ and His Bride… His Church.

There is a bigger picture. Through this teaching we will come to understand why marriage is under attack in our society. Marriage is a sacred institution that God ordained, and it represents Him and His Bride. And, I want to remind you what God's Word says, *"God will not be mocked"* (Galatians 6:7).

A TIME OF PREPARATION

Now, just think about how long it takes a bride to get ready for her wedding day. It takes at least a good year for a bride to get everything ready for her wedding day, right? She's picking out everything: bridesmaid dresses, flowers, venues, etc. etc., because she wants everything to be just perfect. So she's going through all this planning and preparation and the bridegroom just has to stand by and wait patiently for her to get ready. But, on the wedding day, all of the planning and preparation pays off as the bridegroom sees his beautiful bride coming down the aisle towards him. That's a picture of what's going on in the Spirit realm right now as the Bride of Christ is getting prepared for her wedding day. Christ is waiting for her preparation to be completed so He can finally take her as His own. He's waiting for the day when she will walk down the aisle towards Him and He will make His vow to her, and kiss her, and become One with her.

My husband, John, and I have now been married for twelve years. After you've been married to one another for several years you can just look at one another, without saying a word, and you know what each other is thinking. That's because you've *become one*. Can you imagine the Church no longer needing to get a prophetic Word for direction? No longer straining to hear His voice? Instead, she just instinctively knows what the Lord is saying by the way He looks at her, because they are One… because they have spent so much time together, looking deeply into one another's eyes. She's a Bride that is One with her King. She knows what He wants. She flows with Heaven. The struggle of *playing Church* is over!

Now, the Apostle Paul wrote two apostolic prayers in the book of Ephesians. I believe these were prayers for the end-time church. They were actually bridal prayers, whether Paul knew it or not. Look what he prayed for the Church in Ephesians 3:17. He prayed that *"Christ may dwell in your hearts through faith; that you, being rooted and grounded in love…."* Did you catch that? *Rooted and grounded in love!*

A LOVE AFAIR

Most of us aren't there yet. We're not rooted and grounded in love. If you look at the Church, the Body of Christ as a whole, the congregation just sits there, Sunday after Sunday, not rooted and grounded in the love of God. They go to church, they attend a service, they sing songs, they hear a message, and they go home. They're not rooted and grounded in love. They're not in a *love affair* with their Lord and King. They're not walking side by side with their King, seeking Him for what He wants them to do for the day, for their region and for His kingdom. We need to see ourselves as being one with our King, walking hand-in-hand, partnered with Him, worshipping Him, and feeding His sheep, just as the Shulamite woman becomes one with her king and goes out with him into the vineyards.

You see, it's a Divine partnership. Marriage is to be a partnership. It's not that we have a God up in Heaven who is sitting on a throne, and we are His little peons here on Earth. That's what religion wants to convey to you. Religion wants you to think that way so you will stay in the place of control, in a place of subjugation, instead of working hand-in-hand with your King, doing His work in your region. He wants us to be working with Him as His Bride, battling together and taking land for His Kingdom.

THE BRIDE TAKES THE HUSBAND'S NAME

This brings up another way in which the world has perverted the meaning of marriage. It's gotten to the point where the bride doesn't even take her husband's name anymore. Do you see this as a strategy of the enemy, because that's what it is. It's a strategy to minimize the effectiveness of the Bride of Christ. When I married my husband, John, I said, "Honey, you gave me your name. Now I'm a Valencia." That's an honor for a man to give a woman his name. As the Bride of Christ, we have been given the Name! It's the Name above all Names. At the name of Jesus every knee must bow and every tongue must confess that He is Lord!

You see, now I have Jesus' credit cards. Do you understand what I'm saying? I now have *carte blanche*! HaHa! When I became the Bride of Christ, I took on His name and now I have access to the things that I didn't have access to before. When I used to teach ladies' groups, back before Donald Trump became president, I'd say, "What would it mean to you if you had Donald Trump's credit cards?" Since he was a well-known multi-millionaire, all the ladies could relate to this illustration. "I could buy anything I wanted to buy and go anywhere I wanted to go. All I'd have to do is just say, 'Here's his credit card' because it has his name on it."

"I'M MRS. JESUS CHRIST!"

The name represents the person. Behind that name is all that they are, all that they have and all that they do. So, the Church at this hour must rise up to the position of Mrs. Jesus Christ! Hopefully the men can take hold of this thought without getting stretched too much, but we are married to the King of Kings and the Lord of Lords, so when He says "Go" I go. And when He says "Do" I do. And He says, "Not only am I giving you My Name, I'm also giving you My Authority!" You see, with the name comes all the authority that goes with that name. So when we speak the name of our Husband, Jesus Christ, everything has to line up… everything has to obey!

While teaching a group of women several years ago I said, "When you walk into a room, walk in like you own it." Well, you can't do that unless you know who you are married to. I'm married to the guy who owns the building. That means it's mine! This will affect your prayer life. It will revolutionize your prayer life, because God said, "Every place the sole of your foot goes, beloved, sweetheart, my wife, my bride, I've given to you." Do you think when Melania Trump walks into Trump towers she has to worry about if they're going to let her in or not? I don't think so! I carry the name that represents the man I'm married to. Oh! Hear this beloved. This will take you from a formal relationship to an intimate one. It will take you from a weak, wishy-washy Christian to a strong triumphant warrior in Christ.

People sometimes ask me why I have the authority I walk in. The answer is simple… I know who I'm married to. I never question it. I never doubt it and I don't shrink back from it. This must become a part of your DNA. Once it does, you will never feel like a nobody ever again. You will have something rise up inside of you that says, "I am Mrs. Jesus Christ. He liked me so much that He put a ring on it." He sealed the deal. Actually, one of the translations for "It is finished" uttered by Jesus while He was dying upon the cross, is the phrase "It's a Bride" or "I have purchased a Bride." It's a *done deal*. Your vows are sealed with the blood of Jesus Christ!

For a moment, I want to take you back to the year 2006. This was before I got married, and I was praying about teaching this message on the bridal paradigm for the very first time. While I was in prayer, God gave me a vision. He actually took me somewhere in this vision. When the vision was over I wrote down the things the Lord had shown me. Now, of course this is me in the vision, and because I'm a woman, men will have to put themselves in my place for a moment to be able to relate to this vision. These are the words that I wrote down after receiving the vision.

THE VISION

"As the vision began I saw myself in a very large throne room. I was bent over kneeling on the floor in a big, beautiful room. This room had marble floors, golden fixtures and a long entrance way leading to the throne. At the head of the throne room was a very handsome, glorious king sitting on his throne. I was kneeling at the entrance to the room. It was then that I noticed my clothing and my appearance in the vision. I was very disheveled. My hair was matted. The gown I was wearing was covered with dirt and was torn. I was a mess. I noticed even my face was dirty. In the vision I realized that I was not self-conscious about my appearance at all because I was in such awe of this king. He was so handsome and beautiful… so royal and glorious. I kept gazing at him, captivated by his beauty. As I kept looking at him I wondered in my heart, "Why won't he look at me?" He acted as if he didn't even know I was in the room. He wouldn't look at me or even look in my direction. I almost felt as if he was ignoring me. This was very heartbreaking and puzzling to me and it saddened my heart.

The next thing that happened surprised me. Two of the king's servants came over to me as I was kneeling on the floor gazing at him. They lifted me to my feet and began disrobing me and bathing me. All of a sudden I was standing in the same place I had been kneeling, but my appearance was completely different. I was beautiful. The servants placed me in a brilliant long white gown with a gold sash around my waist. They placed a crown upon my head, which was now covered with long, beautiful hair instead of matted hair. As I was standing in awe of how I now looked, I noticed now that the king was starting to take notice of me. He actually looked in my direction and gave me a little smile. He then started to watch me more closely. By this time I was getting a little nervous because he began looking intently at me. His interest in me grew as the moments passed.

Then, to my surprise, the king stood. He stood to his feet and extended his hands toward me. I cautiously, but ever so slowly, walked toward him. He had now stepped away from his throne with his hand extended towards mine. He had the most loving smile I had ever beheld. As I walked towards him I could see that his eyes were so comforting. I stretched out my arm and with my hand I reached out to touch his hand. At that moment I instantly felt a warmth come over me. With this warmth I experienced the most security and love I had ever known in my life. I had never felt such peace, ever. I felt as if I was in a safe place where no evil could ever find me. As I placed my hand in his, he led me towards his throne. All I could do was gaze at him as we walked together. I had not even noticed that there was another chair on the throne next to his. He led me to this chair and motioned for me to sit upon it. I took my place on this throne beside my king."

Proverbs 16:15 says, "*When a king's face brightens, it means life; His favor is like a rain cloud in spring.*"

From that place on the throne, as I sat upon it, I began to realize that I was in deep prayer about the bridal paradigm. I was realizing that I was having a vision. I could still feel his hand on mine. I could still feel the security and peace that I had never known. I could still feel his love, and I knew I would never be the same again as I was coming out of that vision.

IMPORTANT SCRIPTURES CONCERNING THE BRIDAL PARADIGM

Now, I want you to take special note of a few scripture verses that correlate with the vision that I received.

Psalm 40:1-3 (NIV)
1 I waited patiently for the Lord; he turned to me and heard my cry.
2 He lifted me out of the slimy pit, out of the mud and mire; he set my feet on a rock and gave me a firm place to stand.
3 He put a new song in my mouth, a hymn of praise to our God. Many will see and fear the Lord and put their trust in him.

Notice that this verse says when we wait on the Lord, He *turns* to us and hears our cry. In this vision I was waiting for the king to notice me… to turn to me. He did not look my way until I had been prepared to meet Him. He made the way for me to be prepared by having His servants cleanse me and clothe me in new garments… new garments that were pleasing to the King.

Revelation 19:7-8 (NIV)
7 "Let us rejoice and be glad and give him glory! For the wedding of the Lamb has come, and his bride has made herself ready.
8 Fine linen, bright and clean, was given her to wear."

This is a time of preparation for the Bride of Christ. In the vision, I was given a beautiful white gown with a golden sash. I went through a time of preparation prior to being brought before the king. *The old* had to be replaced with *the new*. The Lord is returning for a Bride who is without spot or wrinkle, so we must go through this process if we want to be prepared for His returning.

Ephesians 5:25-27 (NIV)
25 Husbands, love your wives, just as Christ loved the church and gave himself up for her

26 to make her holy, cleansing her by the washing with water through the word,
27 and to present her to himself as a radiant church, without stain or wrinkle or any other blemish, but holy and blameless.

This is the Bridal Paradigm. We must see ourselves as the Bride, or Wife, of Jesus. At the end of the vision, the King brought me to His throne and had me sit beside Him on a throne He had prepared for me. We have to begin to see ourselves as the one who sits beside our King, ruling and reigning with Him in this hour. Many of us haven't entered into His throne room yet. Many of us are still wearing yesterday's garments. Many of us are soiled and disheveled with sin. Yesterday's wineskins will not contain the glory of His Bride in this hour. Many of us want to come into the presence of the King but without proper preparation and attire.

WHAT ARE YOU WEARING?

In Matthew 22:11-14 we read about a wedding banquet being held by a king, and this king noticed that one of the guests was not wearing the proper wedding attire. Do you remember this story? That was not good. The king asked this person, "How did you get in here without *wedding clothes*?" Notice that He didn't say, "How did you get in here without a *church face*? Or *church attire*. He said *wedding clothes*. This man was tied up hand-and-foot and was thrown outside the banquet. So, I want to ask you today, "What are you wearing?" What kind of garments do you have on? The Bible talks a lot about clothing. Jesus eluded to clothing in many of His parables. The Lord provides us with garments to wear, but many of us are still wearing the shame of yesterday. We're not walking in the purity and beauty of the Bride. Instead, we're hanging our heads in defeat, shame, rejection and disgrace. God wants us to make the transition between the old garments we once wore, to the new garments He's provided for His Bride. Have you been cleansed by the washing of His Word? (Ephesians 5:26). Or, do you still feel dirty?

THE WAY THE KING SEES YOU

When I first came to Christ I felt dirty all the time because I didn't yet have the revelation that I was pure, cleansed and spotless. When we go through certain things in our lives it can make us feel dirty and defiled, but that doesn't mean that we are. It's not about how we see ourselves… it's how the King sees us. We've got to learn to see ourselves the way He sees us. Royal, majestic, glorious, powerful, strong! As we read further along in the Song of Solomon we will see what the king says about the Shulamite woman. He says, "*Your neck is like an ivory tower*" (Song of Solomon 7:4). Well, you might read that and say, "What in the world does that mean?" You see, this woman's image of herself was not good, so she probably held her head low… embarrassed by her disgraceful appearance. Yet, the king saw her as one who should hold her head high, like a tower. No words are wasted in this book. Everything has meaning. He said her neck was like a tower, and he was going to hang gold upon it.

In another place in the book, reference is made to their wedding bed. It says, "Our bed is verdant." Do you know what that means? Verdant means it's green, fresh, and growing. It's full of life! A lot of churches today don't have a verdant bed. They're full of corpses. The king's marriage bed had been lined with love. It's purple. It's royal. It's gold. It's majestic. The scriptures elude to the fact that the king had hand-carved his wedding bed in preparation for his wedding day. Listen, Jesus has carved a wedding bed, but He has a Bride who doesn't want to get in it!

A RED-HOT LOVER!

I don't want to be that kind of bride. I don't know one man who wants a frigid, cold bride. Men, you can relate to that, can't you? You want a passionate bride, don't you? You want a red-hot lover! Well, take that over into the Spirit realm. God wants a red-hot lover, not a dead, religious, cold wife. He wants an "on fire" red-hot Bride! A Bride that's not afraid to run into the chamber and get intimate with her lover! You see, some churches say, in deeply religious tones, "Come to the altar, worship Him, come behind the veil," but there's no passion or fire in their voice or heart. They're simply going through the motions. There's no intention of entering into a deep intimate relationship with the Lord… they're just being religious. That's what a cold, frigid bride looks like. The Lord is not coming back for a cold, frigid Bride!

Now, I opened up by sharing from Song of Solomon 1:2, "Oh, let him kiss me with the kisses of his mouth." Initially, that verse may have made you squirm a little, but I hope now you want to kiss Jesus. He wants to kiss you! You see, we think of it in a natural, worldly, soulish mindset… a man, kissing me. That's not it. We're talking Spirit to spirit. When Jesus opens up revelation to you of how much He loves you, it's just like being kissed in the spirit.

FIRST KISS

When you got saved, that was your *first kiss*. That's when you first fell in love. It started a love affair. And when you received the Baptism of the Holy Spirit, you went into a make-out session! HaHa!

Now, think back to your very first kiss. I'm speaking of the natural, worldly first kiss here. Do you remember that feeling? Fireworks were going off. You felt like you could take on the world. Love was alive! But, somewhere along the way, you lost that spark. That's where the Church is today. We've got a Church that hasn't advanced the Kingdom of God one foot because they're not in love. Let's change that. I want to be riding on that horse with Jesus. I'm in love with Him. It's His Kingdom. He's the King. I do what He says. He says, "There's been some trespassers on my property. Get them off!" And I use His name, flash my ring, show that demonic hoard of Hell the covenant God has with me, and say, "It is written!" I'm married to Jesus. We're in a legally binding contract together. He's given me the authority of His name since

A Revelation of God's Love

I'm His Bride!

So this Shulamite woman says, "Let him kiss me with the kisses of his mouth." Let me ask you a question. Do you go to church on Sunday morning saying, "I can't wait to get there to kiss Jesus?" Do you wake up Sunday morning saying, "Oh, Lord, give me a big kiss this morning?" I doubt it. This was the passionate desire of the Shulamite woman… "Oh, let him kiss me." If you're married, when your spouse walks into the room, have you ever said within yourself, "Oh, just let them kiss me?" You've been waiting on them to come home all day long. You're praying within, "Please don't walk in the door and start reading the mail on the table first. Come, kiss me. I've been waiting for you." With that same thought in mind, can you imagine when you enter the doors of your church on Sunday morning, Jesus saying to you, "You've been gone all week long. I've been waiting on you to come through those doors. Please come through those doors with a kiss!" Do you know what the word kiss means in the Hebrew language? It means "to catch fire." When He kisses you, He wants to ignite you with a passion. He wants you to become ablaze for Him. Why isn't the church on fire? Because they go to church, and have a service, and sing a song, but there's no intimacy… no passion. We need to be set afire by the kisses of our King!

When my husband, John, and I got married, it was the second marriage for both of us. I told everyone in that room, "I am the happiest bride you've ever seen." We danced every dance. I don't think we missed one. It was a joyful celebration. During the actual wedding ceremony the minister had to keep reminding us, "It's not time for the kiss yet." We were so looking forward to kissing that we did it before the proper place in the ceremony. They kept saying, "No, wait until the end… wait until we do the vows." We just couldn't stop kissing each other. Do you understand that this is the way Jesus feels about you? Again, the word kiss means "to catch fire." It also means "to love," "to delight in" and "to free." That's huge! The Church is in bondage. They're not free, because they're not in a love affair. But, when He kisses you, you get set free!

When I first taught this message in that Women's Bible Study years ago, there were times when Jesus came into the room so strongly that we couldn't even breathe or move. When that moment would pass, I would say, "We just had a make-out session with Jesus!" To you, that might sound sacrilegious, but remember, I'm not talking about something physical here. So, get out of your physical mindset and see this in the Spirit. He made us this way. He created us for intimacy. When you say, "There's just got to be more than this"… there is! When the world says, "I don't want religion" neither does God. The world needs an encounter. They need the kisses of the Lord. The world needs to walk through the doors of the church and get confronted with a gigantic kiss from their Maker.

Have you ever seen one of those cartoons where somebody gets kissed, then they start spinning and their heart starts beating out of their chest and fireworks start going off? That's how we feel when love is fresh and new. That's how we should leave church… saying, "I'm in love! This is the love relationship between the king and the Shulamite woman we see in the Song of Solomon. So, as we study Song of Solomon just remember that Solomon is the king who represents Jesus, and the Shulamite woman is the one that Jesus is longing for… that's His Bride… that's you and me.

The Bride is not someone who is content with a momentary spiritual experience. She is one who seeks an ongoing, intimate relationship with her beloved. I've seen people come through the doors of my home church, who experience a genuine, heart-felt, intimate encounter with the Lord. They say, "I've never experienced anything like that before." Then, I never see them again. I will never understand that. It's like they're saying, "I've had my ten-year dose of Jesus and that was enough to last me another ten years. Where is the desire? Where is the passion? Where is the hunger? Where is the longing to be with Him? When you're in love with somebody you want to be with them all the time. You count the minutes until you're together again. You can't wait until you see them walk through the door again. In the book of Revelation, Jesus said this to the church at Ephesus: "*I have this against you, that you have left your first love*" (Revelation 2:4).

Do you remember your first love? Do you remember how passionate, how wild, how on fire you were? Can we get back to that place with Him? I don't know about you, but my answer is a definite "YES!"

CHAPTER 2
LET HIM KISS ME

In Chapter 1, I mentioned that the Church knows that it's a Bride, but nobody is living like a Bride. We're not being who God called us to be. So what does God do in such situations? He brings fresh new revelation on something that was always there, something that's always been in His Word, but hasn't been acted upon yet. That's the reason I'm sharing this message of the Bridal Paradigm. Think about it. Where did Jesus perform His first miracle? It was at the wedding in Cana in Galilee. What does that say to you? It says that He loves marriage… He loves weddings… He loves the bride and the bridegroom.

Now, I want to start delving into the first chapter of Song of Solomon, but, before I do that I want to take you to the book of John for a moment. Take note of the following verses:

John 13:23 (NKJV)
Now there was leaning on Jesus' bosom one of His disciples, whom Jesus loved.

John 21:7 (NKJV)
Therefore that disciple whom Jesus loved said to Peter, "It is the Lord!"

John 21:20 (NKJV)
Then Peter, turning around, saw the disciple whom Jesus loved following, who also had leaned on His breast at the supper, and said, "Lord, who is the one who betrays You?"

What did John call himself in all of these verses? *"The disciple whom Jesus loved."* John had a revelation of the love of God. It wasn't that God didn't love Matthew, Thomas, or Bartholomew. It wasn't that He didn't love Peter or Paul. But John knew the love of God in a deep intimate way. It was so life-changing for him that he chose to be identified in that way. Notice that he didn't say, "The disciple who loved Jesus." His own love for Jesus paled in comparison to Jesus' great love for Him. No, instead, he called himself, "The disciple whom Jesus loved." Can you walk there? Can you identify with that?

In Song of Solomon, the very first spoken words we read in Chapter 1 are those uttered by the Shulamite woman as she says, "*Let him kiss me with the kisses of his mouth*" (Song of Solomon 1:2). Those first two words are huge… "*Let him.*" Hear me when I say this… "Let him kiss you." There are so many in the Body of Christ who have either been tainted by religion and traditional teaching, or who have a fear of intimacy and rejection, who think they're doing something wrong if they get too close to God. Listen, if someone ever accuses you of being "too fanatical," more than likely, all that means is you're more on fire than they are.

The scripture is very clear. It says, "*Let him kiss me.*" That means somebody's got to give permission. That means we have to allow something. God gave us all a free will. He never forces Himself on anyone. The Holy Spirit is a gentleman. So, this Shulamite woman cries out from a place of desperation and passion as she says, "Let him kiss me." That's the kind of thing that makes religion run out the door. God says to us through this scripture, "I want a Bride who wants me to kiss her." Wow! That's different than what most of us have been taught, isn't it?

FACE TO FACE

Now, let me share from John chapter 1 using the *The Passion Translation* of the Bible.

John 1:1-2 The Passion Translation (TPT)
1 In the very beginning the Living Expression was already there. And the Living Expression was with God, yet fully God.
2 They were together—face-to-face, in the very beginning.

Now, the phrase "*the Living Expression*" is referring to Jesus. But take special note of verse 2 where it says, "*They were together–face-to-face.*" That's the reason I chose to share from this translation. It puts the relationship between God in Jesus on a more intimate level… a level we don't often think about. They were face-to-face.

Now, go back and read Song of Solomon 1:2 again, "*Let him kiss me with the kisses of his mouth.*" I can't kiss you with the kisses of my mouth if we're not face-to-face. I have to be looking right at you. I have to be right in your face. So, this was written as a love letter from the Lord to His Bride. Some have prophesied over my home state of New Jersey that we are the *Face-to-Face state*. Perhaps this teaching of the Bridal Paradigm will help birth that into reality. Just remember, there's no other way for a bride and groom to truly be intimate unless they are face-to-face with one another.

I shared with you, in chapter 1, that the word "kiss" means "to set ablaze, to set on fire." A kiss is very intimate. When you kiss someone you're not only *face-to-face*, you're also *breath-to-breath*. This Shulamite woman is crying out for the king to come close to her… close enough to feel his breath. Likewise, in our relationship with Jesus, we want Him to come closer to us. We want to tear down the wall of fear and intimidation that stands between us. We want to feel His breath. We desire true intimacy with our King.

I personally haven't seen the church in that place yet, but I know God is taking us there. God wants a passionate Bride. He wants a Bride who is a red-hot lover… on fire for Him…. set ablaze for Him… longing for His kiss. He doesn't want a Bride who is cold, religious, traditional and dead. When you pursue God in that kind of way some will reply, "Oh, you're just being a fanatic." Take that as a compliment, because what they're really saying is, "You're more on fire than me. You're closer than I am."

ABOUT THE AUTHOR, ABOUT THE BOOK

Now, I want to explain a little more about the book Song of Solomon to you. It's written, of course, by Solomon. But keep in mind as you read this story that Solomon (the king) represents Jesus. Although this is a true story about the love affair between King Solomon and the Shulamite woman, there is an underlying theme of the love affair between Christ and the Church.

King Solomon actually wrote three books in the Bible: Proverbs, Ecclesiastes and Song of Solomon. He wrote one thousand and five songs, but this book is given the name Song of Songs, which means that it's the greatest of all the songs he wrote. It is also the only book that Solomon wrote where he doesn't mention his father David. That's because he's writing from a different perspective in this book. He's not writing from the perspective of "the son of David." He's writing from the perspective of "Christ our King."

As I mentioned in chapter 1, this book is a prophetic end-time book. It is written to the end-time church and goes hand-in-hand with the book of Revelation. The book is only eight chapters long, so I recommend that you read it over and over again, in tandem with this book *The Bridal Paradigm*, to get a better grasp on its prophetic meaning. This book records the interaction and love affair between King Solomon and the Shulamite woman. She was a peasant girl. Although Solomon had 700 wives and

300 concubines, this Shulamite woman had a special place in his heart because of the passion she had for him. The fact that she cried out, *"Let him kiss me"* made her his favorite. Let's pull that over into the Spirit realm just for a moment. There are lots of churches, and lots of Christians who are in relationship with the Lord. But listen… *He has favorites.* I want to be His favorite! I want to be the one that holds a special place in the King's heart because of my passion for Him… because I'm willing to meet Him face-to-face, to receive the kisses of His mouth.

INTERPRETATIONS OF THIS STORY

There are several ways that this story can be interpreted. The first way is the physical interpretation.

PHYSICAL INTERPRETATION

With the physical interpretation, we take the story at face value. We consider just the basic facts of the story. It's a true love story. It's an actual, factual account of the love affair between King Solomon and the Shulamite woman who worked in the vineyard. So, in the physical interpretation we basically look at the Song of Solomon as a historical book. But, there is more than fact and history contained in this book. This leads us to the second interpretation.

ALLEGORICAL INTERPRETATION

The second way we can interpret this book is as an allegory. When we say something is allegorical, we're implying that there is symbolism behind the characters, events and facts recorded in the book. We could simply read the Song of Solomon as a nice love story, which is fine, but if we look more closely, we find that there is a deeper meaning than meets the eye.

There is symbolism to be discovered throughout this book. For instance, on the surface we read about the love between King Solomon and the Shulamite woman. But on a deeper level, this book relates to the love God had for the nation of Israel. Throughout the Old Testament, you will read time and again about God's great love for His people, Israel. This book reflects that love He has for her. So, that's the first way it can be interpreted allegorically.

Another way to interpret this book allegorically is to see the king as Christ, and the Shulamite woman as the modern-day Church (the Bride of Christ). It shows God's love for all who have received salvation through the shed blood of Jesus Christ. We find that God not only loves the nation of Israel (the Jews), but also the Gentiles (people of all nations, tribes and tongues). So, not only is this story an allegory of God's love for Israel, it's also symbolic of Christ's love for the Church. It's important to keep this in mind while reading this story.

PERSONAL, PROPHETIC LEVEL INTERPRETATION

The third way we can approach the interpretation of Song of Solomon is on a more personal, prophetic level. In this approach the king represents God and the Shulamite woman represents the individual believer. This is the way that God loves each of us *personally*. Now, this is the approach we're going to take in interpreting the Song of Solomon in this book. Yes, God loves Israel. Yes, God loves the whole Church. But, we've got to learn how to take hold of God's love for ourselves. When I was growing up in the Catholic church I knew that God loved the whole world. He was *Savior*. But it wasn't until I accepted the love of God into my own life on a personal level that I got saved.

The same thing holds true for Song of Solomon. Until I approach this book as God's love song to me it will not transform my life. It will not change me. I've got to have the mindset that this is going to change my relationship with the Lord and cause me to fall in love with Him more deeply. He can't love *me* more. He *is* love! When I get near God I am engulfed in love. He is perfect love. That's where a lot of us get stuck. Our little, finite minds can't comprehend infinite love. That's because we have imperfect, human love.

He's the One you always looked for. He's the One you always longed for. Mommy didn't love you perfectly. Daddy didn't love you perfectly. Your ex-spouse didn't love you perfectly. Even your best friend didn't love you perfectly. People have "come and gone" in your life, and many have hurt you, because human love is an imperfect love. But God's love is perfect love. He overlooks our flaws and inadequacies. He loves us in spite of ourselves.

Can we get to that place where we see ourselves the way He sees us? That's huge! It will change our relationship with Him. It will change our prayer life. We won't be *begging God* in prayer. We won't be looking for some kind of an angle where we're trying to make something happen. We're just stepping into what already is… what already exists. As Christ's wife, we're simply enforcing what He wants us to do, as we use His name to bring change in our life and in our world. There's only a handful of believers who have really taken hold of this revelation. The rest of the Church is *striving to become something*, instead of just realizing who they already are… *we're a purchased Bride*!

Near the end of this book I'll be integrating the Bridal Paradigm teaching into our modern wedding ceremony, as well as the traditional Jewish wedding ceremony. We'll come to understand the true meaning of Jesus purchasing us with a price as we talk about the dowry that was paid in the Jewish wedding. There was a price to be paid. When they made a covenant it was a betrothal. In Hosea it says, "*I will betroth you to Me forever*" (Hosea 2:19). Those words were not only spoken by God to the nation of Israel, they are also spoken by Jesus to His Bride. The Church is in a betrothal period right now. We're betrothed to our beloved Lord, Jesus Christ. In the Jewish tradition a betrothal was just as good as a marriage contract. It's not like engagements of today, which can be made and then broken… on again, off again. No! When God says, "I will betroth you to me forever," it's a done deal. We're essentially already married. All we're doing now is waiting for the actual marriage ceremony, which will take place when the King returns for His Bride.

In the gospel of John, Jesus said, "*I go to prepare a place for you… that where I am, there you may be also*" (John 14:2,3). He was speaking to the disciples. They understood this was a reference to the Jewish wedding ceremony. You see, after the betrothal contract was made, the bridegroom would go off to build the bride a home. He would say to her, "When our new home is ready I will come back and get you." That's what Jesus promised us. He says, "Right now I'm building a home for you, and I will come back and get you when it's completed." Ah! That should bring fresh light to your relationship with Him. You and I are in a love affair with Him. It's a divine partnership where two truly become one. We're not serving Him like a slave. The slave mentality is gone. No, instead, we're the Bride… we're the wife. And, not a subservient wife either. We're a wife that walks hand-in-hand and side-by-side with our King as we rule and reign with Him in this life. We are His representatives here on this Earth.

THE AUTHORITY IN THE NAME OF JESUS

The enemy doesn't want you to get hold of this revelation because, if you do, you'll walk in a whole new level of authority. Yes, there's a new level authority awaiting those who understand that they are now *Mrs. Jesus Christ*! When He says, "I want you to take that land, take this territory in My Name," we go out with His authority to enforce what He's told us to do. We've read about the authority in the name of Jesus hundreds of times in the Scriptures, but now it takes on new meaning as we realize we're walking in the authority of our husband. You see, I'm walking in the authority of my earthly husband as Mrs. John Valencia, but in the Spirit realm I'm *Mrs. Jesus Christ*. I tell John often that he will always be number two in my life as long as Jesus is number one, and he likes it that way. Every husband wants a wife who's strong in God. They don't want a weak, whiny, needy, clingy, wife! Women need to rise up to the place God sees them, just like the Shulamite woman in the story. Solomon said her neck was like a tower. When a woman doesn't know who she is, she'll walk along with her head hanging down. But this Shulamite woman held her head high. She came to know who she was as she saw herself through the king's eyes. When you know who you are it creates confidence inside of you.

So, let me re-emphasize that we are interpreting this book on a personal, prophetic level. As such, we must receive revelation from the Spirit of God to see how it pertains to us. Listen, I can tell you a million times that you are the Bride of Christ, but when you get this revelation from the Holy Spirit, you'll start realizing your true identity… you'll stand taller… something will rise up inside of you.

A PROPHETIC CONTEXT

Earlier I mentioned that a lot of people avoid reading and studying Song of Solomon because they're afraid of it. There is very intimate wording in this book that makes some people uncomfortable. The word *breasts* appears several times in this book. Some people say, "Oh! We shouldn't say that word. It's too sexual… too explicit. We should be talking about God, not about sexual body parts!" Well, let me put that argument to rest. First of all, God created man and woman, and they are sexual beings. When a man and his wife are intimate with one another she conceives and is impregnated. When a pregnant woman gives birth she will bear what? Children. Sons and daughters. Those children will need to be nurtured with milk from their mother's breasts. So when you read about *breasts* in the Song of Solomon don't read it in a sexual context. The mention of her breasts shows that she is mature and is able to nurture children. Near the end of Song of

Solomon this Shulamite woman has completely matured in her relationship with the king, and now she is able to feed sons and daughters from her abundance. Likewise, the mature Bride of Christ is able to feed nations for her King.

In one place the king says, *"Thy navel is like a round goblet… thy belly is like an heap of wheat"* (Song of Solomon 7:2, KJV). Now, that throws some people off. Thy navel? Thy belly? Why the mention of these body parts? Again, don't read this in a sexual or physical context. Read it in a prophetic context. Wheat symbolizes harvest. Her womb was filled with the harvest… a harvest of souls for God's kingdom. There is so much prophetic symbolism in this book that will unfold as we study it.

THREE MAIN CHARACTERS

Now, there are three main characters in this book, so I want to go over that just to bring clarity to who is speaking in the different parts of this story.

The first character is *the beloved*. The beloved is the male voice. This is the masculine voice. It is the voice of King Solomon. But, remember there is prophetic meaning to these scriptures as well, so the male voice is also the voice of God speaking. I love how the New International Version translates the word beloved. It uses the word *lover*. That will take you out of your religious mindset for sure! Have you ever called Jesus "Lover?" We're comfortable calling Him Lord, Savior, and even best friend, but He says, "I'm your lover." If you are His wife, then He is your lover. This takes your relationship with Jesus to another level. It takes you to another place… a place some people don't really want to go. I want to go there, though! I don't want to be anywhere else! I've been in religion and tradition before, and I'm never, never going back.

Now, the second character in the Song of Solomon is the Shulamite woman, and this is the female voice. This is also the Bride of Christ in the prophetic interpretation. So when the Shulamite woman is talking, that's me and you, the Bride of Christ, talking to and about our King. Yes, we are the Shulamite woman. We're the ones who brought nothing to the table. We had nothing to give this King. Solomon, who was the richest person to ever live on the face of this planet, pursued this woman who had absolutely nothing. That's our love story. We had nothing to give Jesus… nothing!

In the days of the Billy Graham crusades, he would end each meeting with an altar call and would sing the well-known song *"Just As I Am."* "Just as I am without one plea… O Lamb of God I come." When I got saved that was my prayer… it really was! I had nothing. I got on my knees and said, "I give you everything… this great big mess in my life… that's all I have that I can give you." What an exchange! And then I became His Bride. It was like marrying the richest man in the world. I went from "rags to riches!" That's what happens when we come to Christ.

Now, I mentioned that the New International Version changes the name of the king from *"beloved"* to *"the lover."* Interestingly, the New International Version calls the Shulamite woman *"the beloved."* So, prophetically speaking, God is *the lover* and we are *the beloved*. So, you and I are *"the one whom Jesus loves."* Does that sound familiar? That's the same terminology John used to describe himself in the book of John. Yes, John understood the Bridal Paradigm. He knew he was the Bride of Christ.

The third group speaking in Song of Solomon is the daughters of Jerusalem. They're the friends of the Shulamite woman. They're the onlookers. In the prophetic interpretation, they are the people all around us in our everyday lives. Some of them are encouraging us, while others are critical of us. So, you see, in the Song of Solomon, if the character speaking is not the king, or the Shulamite woman, then it's the daughters of Jerusalem… the people who are around us. They're the ones that are making comments to us about our relationship with God. They're the ones who say, *"Where did your lover go"* (Song of Solomon 6:1). They're the ones who say to us, "If you and God are so close how come you're going through this difficult time right now? How could He let this happen to you?" So, this Shulamite woman had to contend with these daughters of Jerusalem who often mocked her. And you thought you were the only one who had naysayers in your life! Ha! But these daughters of Jerusalem are in there for a reason, and the Shulamite woman handles their criticisms quite well.

She actually provokes them to jealousy to the point where they want a relationship with the king too. I love that! They actually come to her and ask, "How do I find this king? What do I do?" And she replies, "Follow the path of the sheep." In another place she says, "I'll bring him to my mother's house… the one who bore me" (Song of Solomon 3:4). In the prophetic interpretation, this points to the place where you were born again. That's the church! The path of the sheep refers to the people of God. She's telling them that if they want the king, they must follow in the path of the people of God… His Church… His Bride.

So, you can see that everything in Song of Solomon has prophetic undertones. Everything means something more than what meets the eye. So, there's no need for us to be afraid of this book. If God wrote this to His end-time Church, to His end-time Bride, He doesn't want us to be afraid of it, or to stay away from it.

SOLOMON MEANS "PEACE"

All that I've shared up to this point has been an introduction to this study of Song of Solomon. Now that the groundwork has been laid, we're ready to start from the beginning in Song of Solomon 1:1.

Song of Solomon 1:1 (NKJV)
The song of songs, which is Solomon's.

Chapter one and verse one makes mention that this book is written by Solomon. Solomon means "peace." It carries the connotation of being safe, both in body and soul. When you meet your King you experience a peace you've never had before. It's a peace that restores your soul and body. The name Solomon also means "to be liberated, to be set free." Isn't that what Jesus did for us?

It's interesting to note that the woman's name, Shulamite, and the name "Solomon" are both taken from the same Hebrew word. They have the same root word. "Shulamite" is the feminine version of the word and "Solomon" is the masculine version of the word. Both names come from the exact same place. It means the two are one. It's like we were only half of who we are supposed to be and then God comes along and gives us our other half.

Song of Songs actually means "The greatest song." This is the greatest song that Solomon wrote. He wrote Proverbs and Ecclesiastes, but this was his greatest work. I mentioned earlier that this is the only book Solomon wrote where he doesn't mention his father David. That's because he's writing about somebody else. Revelation 19:10 says *"The testimony of Jesus is the spirit of prophecy."* This book is a prophetic book and the spirit of prophecy is upon it, so this book is the testimony of Jesus. He has given us His testimony and He wants us (His wife) to represent Him and speak on His behalf. When the president's wife goes to another country and steps off the plane, who is she representing? She's representing her husband (the president) and the nation. Well, wherever we go, we represent our husband (Jesus) and His kingdom. My goodness, that's powerful!

Now, when you study the life of Solomon and his kingdom, you discover that his reign was one of peace and prosperity. Listen, when you "get married" to Jesus you come into a new place in your life that you've never been before. You're in a place of peace. You may have come out of a war zone. Some reading this might still be fighting in that war zone, but you're coming out of it. Jesus doesn't leave you there. He pulls you out and brings you into His kingdom of peace. You'll leave a household of strife and come into a new place He's prepared for you. He also brings you into a place of prosperity and provision. That was the hallmark of Solomon's reign. When you're the wife of the king you lack nothing. We have to start thinking and acting like we are married to the King.

GOD WANTS TO KISS YOU!

Song of Solomon 1:2 (NKJV)
Let him kiss me with the kisses of his mouth—For your love is better than wine.

In verse two, the Shulamite woman says, "*Let him kiss me with the kisses of his mouth*." Well, first of all, if He kisses you with the kisses of His mouth, that's the breath of God breathing into you. That's Him breathing His life into you. There's a worship song that says, "This is the air I breathe, Your very word, spoken to me." The word of God is God-breathed (2 Timothy 3:16). When I'm speaking to you I can't separate my words from my breath. When Jesus speaks to us, when His Words leave His *lips*, this is one of the many ways He kisses us. His Word spoken to us is Him kissing us "with the kisses of His mouth."

There are other ways He kisses us, too. Think about mouth-to-mouth resuscitation. Before we met the Lord, we were dead in our trespasses and sins. When we got born again, God essentially gave us mouth-to-mouth resuscitation. He breathed His life into us, much like He first breathed life into Adam in the beginning. You and I were like that man in the story of the Good Samaritan who was beaten by robbers on the road to Jericho. He was left half-dead… bleeding on the side of the road. The Lord came along and breathed His life into us.

Yes, just like He breathed life into Adam, He's done the same to us. That breath came from His mouth. His Word spoken to our dead spirits brought us life. I need His Word spoken to me. I need the kisses of His mouth. Sometimes He speaks to us with the words, "I love you" and that's a kiss from His mouth. Maybe you've had a hard day, the kids have been wild and your spouse is driving you crazy, but you get in your prayer closet and He says, "I love you. Here's my peace." You receive His kiss. You receive His breath. You're at peace.

Maybe you've had a rough week. Nothing has been going right. You're ready to give up. But, you go to church Sunday morning, sit down in your chair and just pray that you'll receive something to help you make it through. His Spirit comes to you as you pray and begin to worship Him. The kisses start coming. All of a sudden you feel the anointing of the Holy Spirit and something lifts off of you. Something breaks. You're in the atmosphere of His presence. His kisses are flowing to you. Then the minister shares the Word of God and His breath is breathing on you, resuscitating you. Those are kisses from the Lord's mouth. I like to say it this way: "When you're in one of those anointed services where the Holy Spirit is really flowing, that's like a Holy Ghost makeout session. In those moments it's like we're making love to our King. That's what worship is.

It's like God is saying "Come into the bridal chamber with me, behind the veil. Come all the way in." You've heard about the outer court, the inner court and the Holy of Holies. Most of the church in America today is in the outer court. They're just spectating from a safe distance. Very few dare to go to the inner court, and God forbid that anyone should presume to go into the Holy of Holies! Stones will be thrown. The people in the outer courts will make fun of you. They'll say, "Who do you think you are! You're a fanatic!" I'll tell you who I am. I'm a hungry girl. Why settle for the outer courts when God has torn the veil to the Holy of Holies? When Jesus died on the cross, the veil between us and God was torn from top to bottom. God ripped it and said, "I want you to come in here. I'm ripping the veil so you can come be with me."

HOW DO YOU RESPOND TO JESUS?

Let's suppose my husband, John, calls me from work and says, "Honey, I'm taking you out tonight. Get all dolled up and I'm going to wine and dine you." All day long that's all I'm going to think about. I can't wait for the moment when he gets home, and when he walks through that door I'm going to be there waiting for him saying, "Let him kiss me with the kisses of his mouth!" That's the way a wife should respond to her husband.

How do you respond to Jesus? You're His wife. We're so afraid of being intimate with Him. The Holy Spirit wants to work in our lives and enlarge our capacity to receive this love. He wants to change our religious mindset. We've been so cold. We've been like an igloo. Our church services have been so cold that we need to distribute blankets as people enter the doors. But the Holy Spirit wants to set us ablaze with the kisses of His mouth.

If someone kisses you that means that you've received favor from them. It restores justice to your life and brings you peace. When Jesus kisses you it means you've received favor from the King, and that will bring freedom and justice to your life. Life can be unfair. Have you figured that out yet? We've all been treated unfairly at one point or another in our lives. But, when Jesus comes into our lives He begins to vindicate us. Do you know why? It's because He says, "That's my wife. How dare you treat her that way! You're not going to rip her off!" Listen. Solomon had 700 wives and 300 concubines, but he loved the Shulamite woman… she received special favor from the king. God loves everyone in the world… but the love He has for His Bride outshines them all!

STRANGERS LIVING IN THE SAME HOUSE

She said, "Let him kiss me with the kisses of his mouth." This is an expectant, passionate response to her king. First of all, she's giving him permission. She's surrendering her will to him. She's saying, "I'm giving you permission to kiss me." The Holy Spirit is a gentleman and must be given permission to work in our lives on this level. You see, even though you're in a relationship with someone, that doesn't mean you're intimate with them. You can have a very superficial relationship with someone even though you may live in the same house with them. There are husbands and wives who live in the same house together but they sleep in separate rooms. They're just two strangers living in the same house. Our relationship with the Lord can be just like that.

Many people go to church, go to the house of God, and even though they're "in the same house" with God they're not engaging with Him. There's no intimacy. That's the way a marriage can lead to divorce. A couple starts sleeping in separate rooms. They stop sleeping together. They stop talking to one another. They don't do things together anymore. They live in the same house but that's all there is to the relationship. That's not what God wants in His relationship with us. He wants a passionate relationship with us. He wants us to go into the deeper things with Him. He wants us to give Him our deepest affection.

BETTER THAN WINE

Now, she also said at the end of verse 2, "Your love is better than wine." Both are intoxicating. His love and His wine. As we interpret this scripture, we know that wine is symbolic of the Holy Spirit. But even if you look at it strictly in the natural, wine is not just intoxicating… it is also the fruit of the vine. This woman worked in a vineyard. She picked the grapes. She knew how to make wine. As a matter of fact, she knew all about wine. So, when she says "Your love is better than wine," she knows what she's talking about.

I tell drug addicts, "There's no high like the Most High!" Any high this world can give you pales in comparison to the high God can give you. His love is intoxicating. In charismatic circles, you might hear this phrase used: "They're drunk in the Spirit!" What do you think that means? It means that person has been drinking a lot of Holy Ghost wine and they've been kissing Jesus. When you're drunk (in the natural) you don't feel anything. You feel no pain. You stagger around, numb to all your problems. They all seem to go away, for that moment anyway. A similar thing happens when you're "drunk in the Spirit." You don't feel any pain. All your problems don't matter anymore. All that matters is Jesus. And, when you wake up in the morning, you don't have a hangover. You've got Holy Ghost residue, and it's so good! That's because His love is *better* than wine.

MORE KISSES FROM THE LORD

Earlier, I mentioned some of the ways God kisses us. One of the most common ways is by way of revelation. When you pray and seek Him in His Word and something pops off the page and comes alive to you… that's a kiss. All of a sudden you understand something you didn't understand before. You see something that you haven't seen before even though it's been there all along. He just gave you revelation. He just kissed you.

Another way He kisses us is through prophetic words given to us by others who are speaking under the Holy Spirit's anointing. I remember one day a friend of mine called me. She's a minister at another church. She said, "I had you on my heart this morning and was praying for you, and God gave me a word for you." She continued, "There have been many things in the physical and the Spiritual realm that have come against you, but God told me to tell you this. He says, 'You're unstoppable.'" That word was a great big kiss from Jesus. God knew I needed to hear that and He put it in my friends heart to call me up and speak that to me.

Still another way He kisses us is with little moments of divine intervention in our lives. Like when you don't have any money and someone walks up to you at church and gives you a "Hallelujah handshake." Maybe you've never heard of that before, but that's when a brother or sister in the Lord walks up to you with a fifty-dollar or hundred-dollar bill in their hand and gives you a handshake, leaving the bill in your hand. You can't help but say, "Hallelujah" as you see the financial blessing they left in your hand. That's a kiss from the Lord!

Another way He kisses us is with favor. Like when you're up for a promotion at your job, and somebody else was more qualified for the job, but you got it instead because the Lord's favor was upon you. The boss wasn't even sure why he gave you the promotion. He just said, "There's something about you that I like." That's God's favor in action. That's a kiss from God, and we walk in that because we're married to the King.

THE FRAGRANCE OF JESUS

Song of Solomon 1:3 (NKJV)
Because of the fragrance of your good ointments, Your name is ointment poured forth; Therefore the virgins love you.

"Your name is ointment poured forth." There's authority in Jesus' name. There is a fragrance in His name. When we speak the name of Jesus we don't even realize all that happens in the Spirit realm. Demons shriek in fear. Angels stand at attention, and they're going to do what you tell them to do. Why? Because the Bride just used the name of her husband, and that name has authority. Lord, help us to recognize who we are!

Listen, when you get close enough to a person you can smell them. That can be a good thing or a bad thing, depending on who the person is! But, with Jesus it's a good thing. His name is like ointment poured forth. It leaves a good fragrance behind wherever that name is spoken.

I have a sister who lives in Virginia and she experiences an interesting phenomenon… she smells Heaven. You know, when you get into the anointing you can feel the power and presence of God. Well, when she gets in God's presence and the anointing of the Spirit is strong, and the glory of God is permeating the place, she can smell Heaven. We'll be in a worship service together and she starts sniffing, and then she'll look over at me and say, "Do you smell that?" I say, "No," but I sure would like to. There's a fragrance with the Lord that very few of us have tapped into yet.

"DRAW ME INTO YOUR HEART"

I want to share Song of Solomon chapter 1, verses 1-4, from the Passion Translation. It sheds a little extra light on what I've already expounded on from these first verses.

Song of Solomon 1:1-4 (TPT)
1 The most amazing song of all, by King Solomon.
2 Let him smother me with kisses—his Spirit-kiss divine. So kind are your caresses, I drink them in like the sweetest wine!
3 Your presence releases a fragrance so pleasing—over and over poured out. For your lovely name is "Flowing Oil." No wonder the brides-to-be adore you.
4 Draw me into your heart. We will run away together into the king's cloud-filled chamber.

Take note of verse 3 where it says, "*No wonder the brides-to-be adore yo*u." That's referring to the onlookers, to those who are not yet saved, to those who are watching your life. He calls them "brides-to-be." Those are the "daughters of Jerusalem" I referred to earlier. They're the ones who have not yet come to know the King intimately through salvation, like you have. But as they see the relationship you enjoy with your King, they are being enticed to enjoy that same relationship on an intimate level. They are brides in the making!

Verse 4 is the Shulamite woman talking. She says, "*Draw me into your heart.*" A lot of us just watch and spectate from a distance. We look at His heart and try to figure it out, but she's saying "*Draw me into it.*"

Some time ago, I received a kiss from the Lord. The kind that I mentioned earlier when someone gives you a prophetic word that encourages you in the Lord. I had just come through ten years of walking through hell on this earth. It was the worst time of my life. I wouldn't wish that experience on my worst enemy. I'll share some of my testimony later in this book, but for now, suffice it to say that it truly was hell for me. After I came through it all, a friend of mine prophesied over me. The things she shared with me were straight from the Father. One phrase she said that particularly grabbed my attention was, "You have walked through the very heart of God."

You know, whenever I think about those words spoken to me I almost cry, because I did… I walked through the very heart of God. I didn't have to. I chose to. I could have gotten hard and went the other way. I could have gotten cold and bitter as a result of the experience. But, I said, "No! I'm going through it with You, Lord." When I did that, I went into God's heart, and being in there gave me the ability to go through it without becoming a bitter, destroyed person. All of those who hurt me and caused me pain, I was able to forgive them, because I was in His heart.

When you got born again, when you said the sinner's prayer, you prayed, "Jesus, come into my heart." Now Jesus is saying to you, "Come into mine!" That changes everything. When you invite Jesus into your heart, you become a Christian. When Jesus invites you into His heart, you become His Bride. That's when "two become one." I'm in my husband John's heart and he is in mine. Nothing can tear that apart. That's why a divorce is such a tearing thing in the natural realm, because the two hearts which had become one are now being torn apart. That's why there is so much pain involved in a divorce.

So, God is calling out to you, for you to come into His heart, so you can be one with Him. Just imagine all that is within His heart! Yet, He is willing to share it with you because… YOU ARE HIS BRIDE!

CHAPTER 3
I AM DARK BUT LOVELY

In this chapter, we're going to talk about the crisis of shame and failure, and we're going to see God's love for us in spite of, and in the midst of, our weaknesses. You see, God didn't wait for us to get perfect before He reached out to us. He sent Jesus while we were still a mess… *"while we were yet sinners, Christ died for us"* (Romans 5:8). So, God doesn't use us in His kingdom because we're so beautiful, because we're so qualified, or because we've got it all together. No, He uses us because we are His! Our identity is wrapped up in Him. This is why the understanding of our identity in Christ is so important.

IDENTITY THEFT

If Satan can steal your identity, hear this, *he can steal your destiny*. Believers who don't know who they are in Christ tend to stay back in their comfort zone… they shrink back from what God is calling them to do. But, believers who know their identity in Christ can be used by God in this final hour. So, Satan is going to work overtime to try and steal your identity. Listen, if you're insecure within yourself, and unsure of who you are, it will be very difficult for you to excel in the gifts of the Spirit. If you lack the confidence of knowing that God is in you, and has called you as His Bride to do His end-time work, you'll be crippled by doubt. "Nobody wants to hear me… I can't speak… I don't even know if I've heard from God or if that was the devil talking to me." These are the kinds of conflicting thoughts that go through your mind and heart when you're unsure of God's calling and gifting in your life. Satan will add to your doubts by planting thoughts in your mind like, "I was bad this week, so God can't use me in ministry," or "I haven't prayed enough or read the Bible enough, so I'm not worthy to be of service in God's kingdom."

TALK TO THE HAND

You can't excel in God if you allow that sort of thing to continue. Here's the secret on how to overcome that… TALK TO THE HAND! That's right. Hold your hand up in the devil's face and just say, "I'm not listening to anything you have to say." The Bible reminds us to "speak to the mountain," and to "prophesy to dead bones." Your voice has got to be louder than that voice of doubt that Satan is speaking to you. When that voice keeps telling you *who you're not*, you've got to use your mouth and proclaim *who you are*… who God says you are. You've got to tell yourself, the atmosphere, and the devil, "This is my identity. I'm the Bride of Christ. I'm His purchased possession. I'm the righteousness of God in Christ Jesus. I may not look like it, and I may not even act like it sometimes, but this is who God says I am. If you have a problem with that, talk to the hand… go talk to Him, don't talk to me!"

So, remember, Satan wants to steal your identity so he can ultimately steal your destiny. Now, the Shulamite woman in this story was looking at the darkness of her outward appearance, but God was looking at her heart. She felt beat down and burnt out. She felt hurt and rejected. All she could see was what the pain and rejection in her life had done to her.

MY PERSONAL IDENTITY CRISIS

I can really relate to this Shulamite woman and the way she felt. You see, many years ago, I was married to a pastor, and we were pastoring a very large, successful church of 1,500 members in Virginia. We were on television and on the radio. Everyone in that area knew me. Things were going along perfectly. But something happened that brought everything to a screeching halt. It was discovered that my husband had been having an affair with a woman in the church, and we lost everything, including our church. I went from being "Pastor Judi," to being "The wife of the pastor who committed adultery."

I went through a tremendous identity shift in my life. I felt dark and stained, just like that Shulamite woman. I could have lived in that. I could have let what happened mark me for the rest of my life. But, I determined that I would fight against those feelings of shame and guilt. I didn't want my identity to be wrapped up in my husband's sin. I didn't want my identity to be shaped by the hurt and shame from that terrible ordeal. I wanted my identity to be wrapped up in who God said I was. Later on, when I married my husband, John, I cried and said, "Honey, you gave me your name. You gave me your name." You see, my last name changed. So much of my own perceived identity was wrapped up in my former husband's last name and I still carried that name with me wherever I went. But, now I had a new name. I became Judi Valencia. I had a new identity. The same sort of thing happens to a person when they become the Bride of Christ. They get a new name and a new identity. Praise God!

Now, long before any of my former husband's indiscretions came to light, there was a guest speaker at our church who prophesied over me with words that didn't fully make sense at that moment. Speaking as God's mouthpiece, they said, "I have called you because your name is Judi, not Turner." (Turner was my ex-husband's last name). You see, God doesn't care what your last name is. He named you. He knows you. He called you. He chose you. Your label doesn't define who you are, nor do the words, comments and judgments of others. Your identity comes from God. Someone might say, "I've been raped." But, that's not who you *are*. "I've had an abortion." That's not who you *are*. "I'm divorced." That's not who you *are*. "I'm widowed." That's not who you *are*!

Satan will try to steal your identity to destroy your destiny, but when you rise up and say, "That's not who I am," you begin to step up in the Spirit. You can't walk in a love affair with the King when you're saying, "I'm just a dirty old yuck!" Your King wants to make you feel like a queen! You undermine what He's doing in your life if your self perception doesn't match what He sees in you.

SPEAK HIS NAME!

Let's look again at some of the passages from Song of Solomon chapter 1, leading up to verse 5.

Song of Solomon 1:3 (NKJV)
Because of the fragrance of your good ointments, Your name is ointment poured forth; Therefore the virgins love you.

When you really love somebody you want to say their name over and over again, don't you? You're so in love with that person that just speaking their name gives you a warm feeling. Well, when we're in love with Jesus, we love to say His name, because our love compels us to do so. "Jesus, Jesus, Jesus." Saying that name brings warmth to the soul. It is like ointment being poured over us. You can feel His love, and His joy when you speak His name. That's what the Shulamite woman is saying in this passage. And because that name brings such warmth, she says, "*Therefore the virgins love you.*" Who are the "virgins" she's referring to? She's talking about those who don't know the King yet… those who haven't come to know Him as Lord… those who haven't come into the Bridal Paradigm. They're the onlookers… those who haven't become intimate with the King. When they see the love that the King has for you, they will be enticed to fall in love with Him, as you have.

THE CRY OF GOD'S HEART

Song of Solomon 1:4 (NKJV)
Draw me away!

As the Shulamite woman reflects on the love she has for her king and for his name, she exclaims, *"Draw me away!"* That's the cry of her heart. But we're going to find out that it is the cry of God's heart, as well. You see, God puts that desire in every one of us. God puts that longing in our hearts to be with Him. Psalm 37:4 says, *"Delight yourself also in the Lord, and He shall give you the desires of your heart."* We'll quote that verse when we want a new car or a new house, but that's not what that scripture means. What it actually means is that God wants us to be so delighted in Him and so open to Him that He can actually place *His* desires inside *our* hearts, so we can fulfill His desire here on Earth.

Song of Solomon 1:4 (NKJV)
Draw me away! We will run after you.

The words, *"Draw me away!"* were spoken by the Shulamite woman. In response to those words, the daughters of Jerusalem say, *"We will run after you."* Now, remember, the daughters of Jerusalem are the onlookers who are watching this love affair between the king and the Shulamite woman unfold. They're saying that as she pursues the king, they're going to follow her.

God has always said to me from day one when I first got saved, "Somebody's got to lead." Somebody's got to go first. So, if you desire more of the Lord and want to grow more intimate in your relationship with Him, there are others who are watching you.

They're paying attention to the way you're living. They're paying attention to the way you're pursuing the Lord… and they will follow you. They'll come and watch you "catch fire." John Wesley said, "Light yourself on fire with passion and people will come from miles to watch you burn." Dry wood catches fire easily. If others are close enough to your fire for the Lord, they will catch fire too.

THIS IS NOT MY CALLING

Song of Solomon 1:5-6 (NKJV)
5 I am dark, but lovely, O daughters of Jerusalem, like the tents of Kedar, like the curtains of Solomon.
6 Do not look upon me, because I am dark, Because the sun has tanned me. My mother's sons were angry with me; They made me the keeper of the vineyards, But my own vineyard I have not kept.

To me, that's one of the saddest verses in Song of Solomon. This woman is so busy tending her brother's vineyard that she has no time to care for her own. On top of that, she's really a shepherdess, not a vinedresser. So, she's being forced to work at something she wasn't called to do. As a result, she becomes burned out and worn down. She was very upset with what her brothers had done to her… with what she was being forced to do. Has anybody ever forced you to do something that you didn't want to do? Has anybody ever forced you to do something you weren't called, equipped or gifted to do? It's a very draining experience. As a result of this misuse of her gifting and calling, she finds herself in a very dark place. She says, "I am dark." She's worn out.

Now, God is drawing us consistently by His Spirit into a deeper, fuller relationship with Him. He's calling us past all the distractions. Past all the hurts. Past all the pain. Past our identity crisis. This Shulamite woman was having an identity crisis. She says, "I'm a shepherdess but I've been forced to be a vinedresser. This is not my calling. This is not who I am."

When I lost my church in Virginia I was co-pastoring a church of fifteen hundred people. Next thing I knew I was an unemployed ex-pastor's wife. I had an identity crisis. I didn't know what to do, or where to go. I was thinking, "How do I start all over? What is God's purpose in my life?" Now, He already told me that I was still called, but I was in crisis. You might be in a crisis at this very moment, but God is always calling us to keep going, to not stop, to press on to His high calling in Christ Jesus. We have choices to make along the way. We can choose to lay down and cry, to curl up in the fetal position and just stay there, or we can get up and go, and follow after God. It's our choice.

"DO I HAVE TO FORGIVE?"

While I was going through this dramatic turn of events in my life, I was blessed to have a very good friend who was an excellent counselor. They became my confidante, because when you're going through something like this you can't just talk to *anybody*. You've got to be careful who you talk to, and who is giving you advice. So, I leaned heavily on this friend during my time of crisis. One of the main things I needed during that time was somebody who would encourage me to stay in a place of forgiveness and not allow bitterness to ruin my life. I was determined that I didn't want this crisis to change my identity into one of a bitter, scornful woman.

While talking on the phone with this friend one day I confessed my anger to her. My anger was justifiable, but I really wanted to overcome it. I said, "It really makes me mad that my ex-husband and this woman ruined my life and my kids' lives, but if I don't forgive them I could go to hell. That's just not fair!" You see, I wasn't as mad about what they had done as much as I was mad about having to forgive them for what they'd done. What she said to me in reply was so very wise, even though I didn't fully understand it at first. She said, "No, you don't *have* to forgive. You have a *choice*, but because of who you are, you don't have a choice."

That was such a good word. She was saying that because of who I am in Christ, because I am identified with Him, I would choose to do the right thing… I didn't *have* to do it… I would *choose* to do it. There's a saying that goes something like this: "If you're going through Hell, don't stop. Just keep on going." I'll always remember those wise words spoken to me because they helped me "go through Hell," and get to the other side. And, now that I've been through this crisis and have overcome, I'm better able to comfort those who are going through a similar crisis.

For many years I had counseled women who were going through divorce and had been cheated on, and I had a measure of compassion for them. But, when I walked it out myself, I had a whole new level of empathy that I never knew before. I could fully identify with their pain, but I was still able to bring them back to their identity, to who they are in Christ. When you counsel others, it helps to be able to identify with what they're going through, but you've always got to bring them back to their identity in Christ and not with the label that they're wearing, or the shame and guilt that they're carrying.

THE TENTS OF KEDAR

Now, back to the Shulamite woman. She said, "*I am dark, but lovely… like the tents of Kedar.*" Now, let's look at the Passion Translation to get a better understanding of the meaning of this verse:

Song of Solomon 1:5 (The Passion Translation)
"*I feel as dark and dry as the desert tents of the wandering nomads.*"

That's pretty bad! Have you ever felt that way… like you're just wandering around in the desert? She felt so dark, and so dry, like she had been in the desert. Her skin was burned and tanned from the scorching sun. That's the way it feels when you don't know your true identity in Christ. The tents of Kedar were made of black-haired skins and they were very, very dark. So, she was identifying with the skins that the nomads used to make their tents. Today, we call these nomads the Bedouins.

There's something else that is very interesting about this verse. Kedar was the name of the second son of Ishmael. What does Ishmael represent in the scriptures? The world... the son of the flesh... not the son of promise. So, she's saying, "I feel dry and burnt, like the son of the flesh." In other words, she's seeing herself after the flesh and not after the Spirit. She's identifying too much with her flesh nature and not with her true identity. Do you ever do that? Do you ever just look at yourself and see only your defects and all that's wrong with you? That's the way she was looking at herself... seeing all of her defects and shortcomings.

Another thing about tents is that they are *outside*. They're not inside. So, she's saying she feels like an outsider... like an outcast. She was out in the wilderness, feeling dark in her soul, seeing only her flesh, identifying only with her sinful nature, not seeing who she is in the Lord.

Also, remember this... the birth of Ishmael was the result of Abraham trying to fulfill the promise of God through fleshly means. He tried to take matters into his own hands. This Shulamite woman was living out the consequences of her brothers taking things into their own hands, and forcing her to do something she wasn't called to do.

THE WRESTLING MATCH IN OUR MIND

Now, if you read Song of Solomon 1:5 in The Passion Translation you will find that this translation attributes portions of the conversation to the Shulamite woman and parts to the king. I believe this is the correct interpretation of this passage, and I'll show you why.

Song of Solomon 1:5 (TPT)
The Shulamite
Jerusalem maidens, in this twilight darkness I know I am so unworthy—so in need.
The Shepherd-King
Yet you are so lovely!
The Shulamite
I feel as dark and dry as the desert tents of the wandering nomads.
The Shepherd-King
Yet you are so lovely—like the fine linen tapestry hanging in the Holy Place.

The Shulamite woman is conflicted within herself and sees the unworthiness of her own flesh, but her king encourages her and shows her what he sees inside her. Do you ever feel double-minded? One moment you're down on yourself and the next you're feeling pretty good about yourself. There's a wrestling match that goes on inside of us concerning our identity. It's a match between the flesh and the spirit. Her flesh says, "I am dark," but the Spirit of the Lord speaks to her spirit and says, "Yet you are so lovely!" There is a battle going on inside of her as she experiences this identity conflict in her life. If you'll be honest, you'll admit that you've experienced this same sort of conflict within. Paul talks about this battle between the flesh and the spirit in Romans 7.

Romans 7:19, 24 (NKJV)
19 For the good that I will to do, I do not do; but the evil I will not to do, that I practice.
24 O wretched man that I am! Who will deliver me from this body of death?

This is the battle that is going on inside the Shulamite woman's mind and heart. She sees herself one way, but her king sees something different. "I'm dark." "But you are lovely." "I'm rejected." "But you are lovely." We've got to start identifying ourselves by the way God sees us, not the way we see ourselves. Many people have a hard time identifying themselves in the Spirit because they keep on looking at the darkness in their life.

Song of Solomon 1:5 (NKJV)
I am dark, but lovely, O daughters of Jerusalem, Like the tents of Kedar, Like the curtains of Solomon.

Now, the curtains of Solomon were in the Holy place, in the temple. They were white, made of pure white linen. So there is this dichotomy going on here: "I am dark… but I'm also lovely. I'm like the dark skins on the tents of Kedar… but I'm also like the pure white linen curtains in the Holy of Holies. Can you see the conflict? Which one is going to be your identity? Which one are you going to align yourself with?

The curtains of Solomon were bright white and were hung in the Holy place of the Temple. The name *Solomon* means "peace." When you're walking in the right identity there is no torment or turmoil. There's peace. "I am who God says I am. I am lovely. I'm pure white linen in the Holy place." These are the confessions of a person who has found their identity in their King, not in their own self.

Those who say, "Don't look at me because I am dark," are seeing themselves only after the flesh… only according to their failures and shortcomings. When I was going through my wilderness experience, many times I felt like saying, "Don't look at me, I'm dark." Adding insult to injury, I had some of "Job's well-wishers" come along as I was going through my own personal hell, and they said, "Well, what did you do to cause all of this?" Truly, it was a dark time in my life, and I had every reason to say, "Don't look at me because I am dark," but God wouldn't allow me to identify myself in that way. God was saying to me, "You're like the pure white linen curtains in the Holy place." So, listen. Your identity isn't wrapped up in what has happened to you or what you've done in the past. Your identity is wrapped up in Him!

The tents of Kedar were outside. The curtains of Solomon were inside, in the Holy place. You're not an outsider. That's not your identity. God sees you as the curtains inside His temple, in the inner court… in the Most Holy Place… in the place where God dwells. There's no identity crisis when you're in God's presence.

Song of Solomon 1:6 (NKJV)
Do not look upon me, because I am dark, Because the sun has tanned me. My mother's sons were angry with me; They made me the keeper of the vineyards, But my own vineyard I have not kept.

This Shulamite woman has a poor self image. She says, "I am dark… don't look at me… the sun has burned me." Have you been "burnt" before? If you're alive and breathing on this Earth, you've most likely been burnt before. You've been ripped off. You've been taken advantage of. You've wanted to say, along with this Shulamite woman, "Don't look at me… don't judge me, because I got ripped off. Somebody burned me." We've all been there before. She says, "My mother's sons were angry with me. They forced me to work in their vineyards." Do you know what that is right there? That's the spirit of jealousy. Have you ever been attacked by the spirit of jealousy before? If you've been in the church even the smallest amount of time then you've probably experienced this. I've experienced it first hand, so I know whereof I speak. "Who does she think she is over there prophesying? Who does she think she is, starting a ministry?" I've heard those accusations stemming from the spirit of jealousy before. It's a mocking spirit.

Do you know what I did for ten years after I lost my church of fifteen hundred people? I became a floral designer. Where does a default pastor's wife go to recover? How does she pay the bills and put a roof over her head? I did what I had to do. I love flowers, so I became a floral designer. I did that for ten years. But that was not my identity! While I was making flower arrangements I was still a daughter of the Most High God. I was still called to do His kingdom work, because my name is *Judi*, not *Turner*. Remember... if you don't know who you are, your identity can be stolen from you.

So, you see, I can associate with this Shulamite woman. She was being forced by her brothers to do something she wasn't called to do. I wasn't called to be a floral designer, but I did it to make ends meet. I felt dark. I had been burned!

MY OWN VINEYARD I HAVE NOT KEPT

Just like that Shulamite woman, and just like me, there have probably been times in your life where you've been forced or coerced into doing things you have no anointing to do. Churches are notorious for doing this. They stick people into positions of ministry because they need somebody to fill a hole. That person may not have any of the gifts, anointing, talent or grace to do that particular ministry. They need somebody in the Nursery or in Children's church, so they'll take any warm body and plug them in the position regardless of whether or not that person is anointed for such ministry. May God help the church to put an end to such practices. People need to be in positions of ministry that are suited to their anointing and calling so they don't feel forced and out-of-place in the Church.

That's what was happening with this Shulamite woman. Her brothers forced her to work in the vineyard. "Let's have her go pick grapes out in the hot sun... turn her fingers purple... turn her skin dry and dark." Now, the worse part about this is that her own vineyard got neglected in the process of taking care of her brother's vineyard. To me, that's the saddest part of this whole story in Song of Solomon. It's sad to see a person being forced into a life that's completely contrary to their calling, having to neglect their own anointing and calling because they are being taken advantage of.

The scripture says that she was rejected by her brothers and that's what put her there. Maybe that's why I relate to this woman so well. I know what it's like to be rejected by "brothers" in the Lord. I was put out of the church in Virginia that my husband and I had founded. I was rejected, not because of something I had done, but because of what my husband had done. I had to neglect my own calling and anointing as I was forced out of that church. Neither I nor my kids had done anything wrong, yet we were being punished as if we had. Now, I have forgiven those involved, and I can say that with all of my heart, but I could write a book on what *not* to do when a pastor has a moral failure. I was a founder of that church, yet I was going through hell because it wasn't just a "one-night stand." The affair had been going on for eight months. They called me into my office, handed me a pre-typed letter of resignation and said, "Clean your office. It would be better for us if you and the kids didn't come back."

Then, that Sunday Night, they had a memorial service. "Moses" was dead, and they were ready to move on to the "promised land" without us. We were forced into bankruptcy. We were forced into becoming homeless, after pastoring a church of fifteen hundred people and everybody in the town knowing us. That wasn't my true identity, but I was definitely going through an identity crisis at that moment. So, I can really identify with the woman in this story as she's being forced to do things she didn't want to do. She was rejected by her brothers... I was rejected by other believers in the family of God.

Do you know what the biggest shock was to me when I first became a Christian? I thought all Christians were supposed to be the most loving, wonderful, beautiful people in the whole world. Right? What a shock! What a wake up call I had! As the saying goes, "It can make you bitter or make you better... it's your choice." I had to tell my kids, "Listen, we have a choice. We can either become like that or we can determine that we are going to be real believers... real lovers... real forgivers." I want to show people what Jesus is really like, even if I have to do it in the midst of a bunch of hypocrites. Amen?

So, here was this Shulamite woman. She's been rejected by her brothers, by other believers in the family of God, being made to work in a ministry that she wasn't called to. All the while she's failing to take care of herself. Have you ever been so overworked that you neglected your spiritual walk with God? In the process, you got so dried up, and so burnt out because you were forced to do something outside of your calling? That's what happened with this woman. She says, "My own vineyard I have not kept."

IN THE WILDERNESS

In Hosea chapter two we find a beautiful love story, similar to that found in Song of Solomon. In verse 14, this is what God says to this woman (and He's saying this to you, as well).

Hosea 2:14 (NKJV)
Therefore, behold, I will allure her, will bring her into the wilderness, and speak comfort to her.

The woman in this story had been darkened by her circumstances, just like the Shulamite woman. But, God said, "I will allure her." The word allure means *to woo, to tug at the heart, to entice.* God sees where she is and wants to allure her away from her dark set of circumstances. Where does he want to allure her? Brace yourself. "Into the wilderness." He said He wanted to speak comfort to her in the wilderness. And, not just any wilderness, mind you. Look at the next verse.

Hosea 2:15 (NKJV)
I will give her her vineyards from there, and the Valley of Achor as a door of hope; she shall sing there, as in the days of her youth, as

in the day when she came up from the land of Egypt.

Achor means *trouble.* He said He would turn her wilderness of trouble into a door of hope. A place where she can sing as in the days of her youth, as in the day when she came up from the land of Egypt. Whenever you see Egypt mentioned in prophetic scriptures it is symbolic of the world. So this is referring to when a believer comes out from the world and comes into God's kingdom. He said that she would sing again, like when she first got saved. Now, nobody wants to go through a wilderness experience. Am I right? But what you have to understand is that this wilderness being spoken of here is, first of all, a place of privacy. He's saying to her, "Come, get alone with me. Something interesting to note is that one of the Hebrew definitions for the word wilderness is "mouth." So, He's saying to her, "Come, get alone with me, to a place where I can speak to you." The wilderness is not a place of punishment. It's a place of privacy. What a difference it would make in our lives if we looked at our wilderness experiences in this way!

God is alluring her into this place of privacy where He can comfort her. It's a place free from distractions and disruptions. It's a place where none of the things that have hurt you or caused you pain can get to you. It's a solitary place. It's a place where God can take all of the trouble away and turn it into hope.

Now, going back to Song of Solomon, in chapter 8, verse 5, it says, *"Who is this coming up from the wilderness, leaning upon her beloved?"* The woman in Hosea went into the wilderness alone, because God was alluring her there... because He wanted her to get away from all the distractions and draw close to Him. Now, in Song of Solomon, we see her coming *out of the wilderness*... not alone... she's leaning upon her lover. She had been transformed in the wilderness. She was healed in the wilderness. She was given back the things that were taken from her. She was once dark and burnt, but now she's filled with hope.

"HUSBAND" NOT "MASTER"

Now, let's go back to Hosea, where we left off in verse 16.

Hosea 2:16 (NKJV)
"And it shall be, in that day," says the Lord, "That you will call Me 'My Husband,' and no longer call Me 'My Master.'"

Oh, that is so good! In the day you come up out of the wilderness, after God has turned all of your trouble into a door of hope, your relationship with Him comes to a brand new level. He allured you into that wilderness for a time of privacy, so He could minister to you without any distractions. His work is completed, and now you're ready to be released out of the wilderness into your new assignment. Your "vineyard" that you neglected has been restored to you. You're leaning on Him, trusting in Him, walking hand-in-hand with Him, serving in ministry with Him. You're no longer His servant. The wilderness experience changed all of that. Now you're something more. You're no longer content to call him, "Master." Now you call Him, "My Husband." No one can label you in a negative way. No one can talk about your past, because the past is gone. You have a new name now! You have a new identity. You are now Mrs. Jesus Christ!

Some people don't enjoy the wilderness. They even rebuke the thought of the wilderness. But, when you see that God calls you there for a time of private intimacy, you change your perception of the wilderness. You no longer despise the wilderness. You no longer reject the wilderness. Instead, you welcome it... you run to it, because you know that is the place where you learned to call Him "My Husband," and no longer call Him "My Master." This is of huge importance, and I'll tell you why.

Religion wants to make you a slave. The Shulamite woman's brothers had made her a slave in their vineyards. Listen, there are times when the church unwittingly brings people into slavery.

We burn people out in church. We make them do things they're not called to do. Some we even overwork because no one else will volunteer. We encourage people to have a "servant's heart" but, many times it leads to a place of subservience. We all want to "serve God," right? But, it doesn't need to be from a legalistic, religious spirit. Many times religion makes us, "Do, do, do, do." We're *doing* but we're not *being*. I don't want religion... I want relationship. I'm in love with the Lord and He's in love with me. Anything I do for Him is out of a heart of love for Him. I'm not serving Him so He will love me more. He's my Husband. He's my Lover. I don't *work* for Him. No! I'm in a relationship with Him. He says to me, "You're not my slave... you're my Bride!"

Listen, King Solomon was a king with a thousand wives and concubines, but he had just one throne next to his, and he said, "This is where you sit, my beloved." Likewise, the Lord says to us, "This is your chair next to me. Not working, not slaving. You carry My Name and you're doing my work as I flow through you. It's not labor. It's not servitude. It's a flow of our relationship." In my relationship with my husband, John, I do things for him because I want to. It just flows out of me because I love Him. I'm not trying to make him love me more by doing things for him. If you're in a relationship with a very domineering, demanding spouse you feel like a slave after a while. You find yourself responding to them with a formal "Yes sir," instead of "Honey, what can I do for you?" There is no loving relationship there. That's not the way our relationship is supposed to be with the Lord, but many, many have it.

GET RID OF THE IDOLS

Now, let's look closer at that scripture in Hosea again.

Hosea 2:16-17 (NKJV)
16 "And it shall be, in that day," says the Lord, "That you will call Me 'My Husband,' and no longer call Me 'My Master.'

17 For I will take from her mouth the names of the Baals, And they shall be remembered by their name no more."

"The names of the Baals." Those are the idols and the other lovers that you once served in your past life. God says, "They shall be remembered by their name no more." Once you've been to that intimate place with the Lord, He wants to remove the thought of your past idols and lovers from your memory. Do we have idols in our society today? Maybe they're not the carved-in-stone type of ancient times, but, make no mistake... idols still exist in our lives today.

I think about how crazy some football fans get during football season. They paint their faces, put on wigs, take off their shirts so they're bellies are hanging out in twenty-below-zero temperatures and yell at the top of their lungs for a bunch of grown men jumping on a pigskin. If you love football that's fine with me, but I've known people who buy season tickets for their team and you don't see them in church until after football season is over. The name of Jesus isn't on their lips. Instead, it's the name of Giants, Jets, Eagles and Cowboys. God want's His name to be in your mouth... not the name of the idols in your life. *"And they shall be remembered by their name no more."*

What are the Baals in your life? I've mentioned that sports can be one, but here's one that you might not have thought about... your own kids. Listen, anything that keeps you from Him, anything that you love more than your time with Him, those things are idols... they are the Baals in your life. The heart of the Bride is to be with the Bridegroom. Nothing else can take His place in her life. She desires His kisses more than anything else. Religion tries to rob us of that place of intimacy with the Lord. In that respect, even religion can become an idol in our lives. Anything that tries to take the place of our intimate relationship with the Lord is a bonafide idol in our lives. He wants only one name to be on our lips. It's not the name of "Religion" or "Theology." It's the name of Jesus! Jesus has got to be number one in our lives. His name has got to be the number one name that comes across our lips.

I tell my husband, "John, you'll always be number two in my life, because Jesus is number one." John is fine with that. In fact, he wants it to be that way in our marriage, just like I want his number one to be Jesus and not me. That's the way every marriage should be. Every husband wants a wife like that, and every wife wants a husband like that. "Go love Jesus, and then come back and love me." Marriages work best that way. Once you've bathed in the love of Jesus then you have more love to share with your spouse.

THE IMPORTANCE OF PRAYER

Do you know who David Yonggi Cho is? He's the pastor of one of the largest churches in the world. His church is in Seoul, Korea and has three quarters of a million members. They have a prayer mountain that has prayer grottos in it and a prayer chapel on top. I got to go there for a church growth conference many years ago. On the weekends there would be ten to fifteen thousand people praying in that chapel, and on the weekdays there would be three to five thousand. We went to one of the prayer meetings at the Olympic Stadium on a Tuesday afternoon and there were over forty thousand people there. They were praying for the reunification of North and South Korea. In years past, that seemed like an absolute impossibility, but in recent years it looks like all those prayers are paying off.

Cho confesses all the success that the church has achieved is due to the prayer that goes up regularly there. He said, "I couldn't do this unless I prayed three to five hours a day." He explained the importance of prayer in humorous fashion, with his thick Korean accent. He said, "Before I go into prayer I might have been in an argument with my wife, so I'm saying, 'Lord, my wife… she's so ugly… she's so ugly.' But after I've prayed for three hours I'm saying, 'Lord, my wife… she's so beautiful… she's so beautiful.'" Prayer changes the way you see things. When you've been face-to-face with God in prayer you begin to see things from His perspective. Prayer really does change things. More importantly, prayer changes you.

So, when we were at this prayer meeting of forty thousand believers, Cho said, "Let's pray." At that moment a "roar in the Spirit" enveloped the building as forty thousand people lifted up prayer together at the top of their lungs. They are very disciplined in their praying. As a matter of fact, the only way he can get them to stop is by ringing a little school desk bell that he holds up to the microphone when the prayer time is over. He says, "If I don't do that, they will never stop. They will just pray and pray all day long."

Do you know what I came back home from Korea with? Shame on America... that's what I came back with. We have all this religious freedom, all the blessings that we have here, and if I call a prayer meeting at my church I'm doing good to get 30 people to show up. I tell the people in my home congregation, "We've got to go from *'have to'* pray to *'can't wait'* to pray if we're going to be effective in prayer." If you've been in that face-to-face encounter with the Lord, you'll run to prayer. You can't wait for an opportunity to get intimate with Him because you're His Bride, and you're going with Him to do His work. You're establishing His kingdom on Earth as His representative. It's not a religious drudgery where He's "Master" so you begrudgingly obey His call to pray. No! Instead, you can't wait to pray, because in your heart you're saying, "I'm doing my beloved's work."

GOD WILL "SOW YOU INTO THE EARTH"

Now, let's look at the last few verses of Hosea chapter 2.

Hosea 2:19-20, 23 (NKJV)
19 "I will betroth you to Me forever; yes, I will betroth you to Me in

righteousness and justice, in lovingkindness and mercy;
20 I will betroth you to Me in faithfulness, and you shall know the Lord.
23 Then I will sow her for Myself in the earth....

Did you hear what God said? He's saying, "I am married to you forever." But did you catch that last sentence? He wants to sow you into the earth! Now that you know Him, now that you represent Him correctly, now that you know you're His Bride, He says, "I want to sow you into the earth, because you are one who will correctly represent Me." Jesus has been so misrepresented to this world by the Church. The world doesn't want your Jesus because you're always calling Him "Master." You're representing Him as a hard taskmaster. They've grown up with religion. They don't want that. What they are looking for is a loving relationship. They want somebody to love them for who they are. They want something real.

So, get ready for green-haired, tattooed, body-pierced people to come to you asking you about your relationship with the Lord, because they want something real. If you've been with the Lord face-to-face and have had an encounter with Him, you can say to them, "Come with me into the wilderness and meet Him there. You may feel alone and rejected now, but when you come out of the wilderness you'll have a restored hope and confidence. You'll not come out of the wilderness alone. You'll be leaning on your beloved. He'll remove the names of the Baals in your life: drugs, sex, immorality, and perversion. He'll remove their names from your mouth. He'll sow you into the earth as a blessing." That's what this world is needing! An intimate experience with the Lord... not a religious experience.

My kids were in a lot of Christian schools when they were growing up. Some of them were good and others were not so good. In one of the schools, they operated like they were the Gestapo. They called the principal "headmaster." I had to pull them out of there. My daughter was beginning to hate church. She was hating Christianity, because it was being misrepresented. Jesus wants to love on everyone, and we're vessels He wants to sow into this earth so they can see His love and beauty flowing out of us.

Hosea 2:23 (NKJV)
Then I will sow her for Myself in the earth, and I will have mercy on her who had not obtained mercy; then I will say to those who were not My people, 'You are My people!' And they shall say, 'You are my God!'"

"And I will have mercy on her who had not obtained mercy." Do you ever just wish someone would cut you a break? I've counseled people before and told them, "You're always the first person to cut others a break. Now, how about cutting yourself a break." We're so hard on ourselves. We beat ourselves up. Well, God says, "I will sow you into the earth for Myself. I will have mercy on her who had not obtained mercy, then I will say to those who were not My people, 'You are my people...'" He will show you mercy even when you won't show mercy to yourself. He wants you to know that He calls you His own, and in return, He wants to hear you say, "You are my God!" That's the desire of God's heart.

CHAPTER 4
FINDING YOUR PLACE AT THE KING'S TABLE

We will start this chapter by looking at Song of Solomon 1:7-17, and I will preface each portion of scripture with just a note about who is talking in each of these verses. So, as we begin reading, the first person talking is the Shulamite woman.

Song of Solomon 1:7 (NKJV)
Tell me, O you whom I love, where you feed your flock, where you make it rest at noon. For why should I be as one who veils herself by the flocks of your companions?

The next words are spoken by the king.

Song of Solomon 1:8-10 (NKJV)
8 If you do not know, O fairest among women, follow in the footsteps of the flock, and feed your little goats beside the shepherds' tents.
9 I have compared you, my love, to my filly among Pharaoh's chariots.
10 Your cheeks are lovely with ornaments, your neck with chains of gold.

Verse eleven is spoken by the Daughters of Jerusalem. Remember, they are the onlookers, those observing this love affair between the Shulamite woman and the king. They also represent those of your family and friends who are watching your personal relationship with the Lord.

Song of Solomon 1:11 (NKJV)
We will make you ornaments of gold with studs of silver.

The Shulamite woman speaks in verses twelve through fourteen.

Song of Solomon 1:12-14 (NKJV)
12 While the king is at his table, my spikenard sends forth its fragrance.
13 A bundle of myrrh is my beloved to me, that lies all night between my breasts.
14 My beloved is to me a cluster of henna blooms in the vineyards of En Gedi.

Then, the king speaks back to her:

Song of Solomon 1:15 (NKJV)
15 Behold, you are fair, my love! Behold, you are fair! You have dove's eyes.

And her response is:

Song of Solomon 1:16-17 (NKJV)
16 Behold, you are handsome, my beloved! Yes, pleasant! Also our bed is green.
17 The beams of our houses are cedar, and our rafters of fir.

Now, I've said before if you just take this scripture in its natural context it can be difficult to understand. It must be interpreted in the spirit realm. When you read, "A bundle of myrrh between my breasts... henna blooms in the vineyards of En Gedi," you might be thinking, "What in the world are you talking about?" Well, first, you have to understand the time and the setting of this story, because this is not a fairy tale. This is an actual true story. It is historical.

I recently visited the Holy Land and was blessed to see so many of the places that are referenced in the scriptures. Everywhere you go, you can see pieces and parts of history. You realize that the Bible is not a fictitious book, but that history backs up everything written in its pages. We went to Mount Carmel where Elijah called fire down from heaven. We went to the place where King Hezekiah lived. We even visited the place where Jesus was resurrected from the dead. Seeing these places first hand gave me an even greater appreciation for the historical value of the scriptures.

A PICTURE OF GOD'S LOVE FOR US

So, we're talking about King Solomon. He was an actual, historical figure. Solomon's temple was an actual, literal, historical place… not the figment of someone's imagination. However, we are not looking at Solomon or the writings in Song of Solomon just for their historical value. We are looking at them as an allegory of God's love for us. We're taking this historical account of King Solomon's love affair with this peasant Shulamite woman and finding end-time revelation for the last days Church.

God does nothing by mistake. There is a reason why Song of Solomon is included in the scriptures. The deep love that Father God has for us is portrayed through this loving relationship between Solomon and the Shulamite woman. The love that is referenced here is a foundation that the Apostle Paul built upon in 1 Corinthians 13 when he proclaimed, "Love is patient. Love is kind. Love bears all things, believes all things, hopes all things, endures all things." Paul didn't get this revelation about God's love on his own. Read through 1 Corinthians 13 and you will find a description of a love that was exemplified in Song of Solomon. If you want a greater revelation of God's love for His Bride, the Church, you must read and study Song of Solomon with greater hunger. Every one of us needs to know and understand this loving relationship that God is seeking to have with us.

Religion keeps us out of relationship. If you've been in church your whole life… if you've been saved for twenty years, but you're not in a loving relationship with the Lord, then you've been in religion… you've missed something. God has something much deeper and richer for us and that's why He's bringing this message of the Bridal Paradigm to the forefront in this hour.

Now, if you recall, I mentioned that the Shulamite woman had neglected her own vineyard because her brothers were angry with her and forced her to work in their vineyards. Not only was she neglecting her vineyard, she was also neglecting her calling, because she was a shepherdess, not a vinedresser. She was used to working with sheep, not with vines and grapes. So, we find her frustrated and burned out from being out-of-sync with her calling and anointing.

When the king finds her, he allures her into the wilderness. He takes her aside to Himself. Why? So he can minister to her. He wants to minister to her in her place of exhaustion, desperation and even woundedness. He drew her into the wilderness so he could speak tenderly to her heart. Remember, the wilderness is symbolic of a place of privacy where God can minister to your heart and restore you. So, this is the setting where this portion of scripture is taking place, as the Shulamite woman cries out in desperation:

Song of Solomon 1:7 (NKJV)
Tell me, O you whom I love, where you feed your flock, where you make it rest at noon. For why should I be as one who veils herself by the flocks of your companions?

Finding Your Place at the King's Table

This is the cry that every person has in their heart at one time or another in their life. It's a cry for rest and peace in the midst of aggravating circumstances. It's a cry that stems from the realization that you have been forced into a situation outside of your control. You feel boxed in and frustrated. It's a place where you're doing things that you don't really want to do, but you seemingly have no choice. It's a place where you realize the only solution is total surrender to God. You see, God doesn't come and whack you with a club and say, "What are you doing all messed up in this place? How did you get here? Why did you let yourself get to this place?" That's what our religious upbringing has told us. It's what wrong teaching and theology have told us. We're told that God is mad at us and will make us go through the wilderness until we repent. But, God is saying, "I'm not mad at you. I love you. I want to restore you. I want to heal you. I've brought you to this private place so I can reveal My heart to you." And, when we see God's heart for us, it makes us want to surrender to Him. Nobody wants to surrender to a tyrant... nobody.

But when we see that we have a loving Father, a loving God, (and in this story) a loving King, that's when we come to that place of surrender. We come to a place where we can ask God for help, because we know that He loves us. Often times, when things are going wrong in people's lives, they tend to run from God and blame Him. In the world, people often say, "How could a loving God allow this to happen in my life?" It's obvious that they don't know this loving God we serve when they make such accusations. They don't realize He had nothing to do with the misfortune in their lives. He hates it just as much as they do. His heart is broken over it. He's the One who came to restore the brokenhearted, and to heal and bind up all their wounds.

THE NEED FOR FOOD AND REST

So, here this woman is asking, "Tell me, O you whom I love, where do you feed your flock?" When someone is asking where you get fed they must be hungry. The first thing we see then is that this woman is in a place of hunger. She also asks, "Where do you make it rest at noon?" She's exhausted. When you do things you're not called to do, like this woman did, it leads to exhaustion. She's hungry, and she's exhausted.

There was a man in my home church who was forced to work on Sundays for several months. He didn't have a choice in the matter. Because he had been out of church for quite some time, he wasn't getting fed spiritually. So, it doesn't necessarily mean you've done something wrong if you're not being fed, or if you're exhausted. Sometimes life circumstances can put you there.

So, she is asking, "Where do you feed your flocks, and where do you make it rest," from a place of exhaustion... she's burned out. But, she's also asking, "God, where are you?" When you get burned out and exhausted you don't seem to be able to feel God's presence anymore. So she's in this place of desperation. She wants to be fed again. She wants to feel God's love again. She wants to feel God's leading again. She's a little mixed up right now because she thought she was doing everything right, but she can tell that something is missing in her life. She's asking God, "Lead me back to where You are... bring me back!"

Every one of us has probably been in that very same place at one time or another. It's not necessarily a bad place to be. At least when you're in this place you realize that something is missing. You're not pretending everything is okay. The missing peace in your heart leads you back to Him. Perhaps you just got so busy in your everyday activities that you neglected your spirit. We've all been there. Life has a way of distracting us from our relationship with the Lord. Then we cry out to Him, "Lord, bring me back to where You are. I just want to be where You are." Life knocks us down sometimes. In my case, I had a church, and a wonderful family... next thing I knew, I had nothing. I knew I still had the Lord, but I cried out to Him, "Lord, you've got to help me find my place, because I don't have it anymore. Where's my place? Where can You feed me? Where can You give me rest?"

She asks, "Where do you feed them and where do you cause them to rest at noonday?" What is noon? Noon is the heat of the day. It's when the sun is at its highest point and strongest intensity. She wants to know where God takes His flock to rest when things get really heated up. She wants to rest there. She wants to be with Him and no one else. She's realizing that He's the only one she needs to follow right now. She tried it her way and it didn't work.

Many of us had to get to the end of ourselves, the end of our own ways, the end of our own thinking, before we would completely surrender to the Lord. As for me, I grew up in the Catholic church. Every church service I'd see Jesus hanging on the cross. Every Saturday I'd go to confession and confess what I did wrong all week long, so I could take communion Sunday morning, and by the time I got in the car Saturday night I had already hit my sister, lied to my mother, and done a lot of things I wasn't supposed to do. So I wasn't experiencing any of God's grace. There was never ultimate forgiveness or mercy. It had become all about works. So, whenever I had troubles or needs in my life it was definitely difficult for me to go to this guy that I had nailed to the cross. I couldn't ask for His help because I was so sin-conscious, I didn't think He'd want to help me. I felt like I still needed to pay for my sins. I wasn't truly forgiven. When you have that kind of perception of God it makes it very difficult to believe that He is on your side. I had a whole lot of wrong thinking about God that hindered me in my relationship with Him until I completely surrendered to Him.

HIDING BEHIND THE VEIL

She asks him the next question:

Song of Solomon 1:7 (NKJV)
Why should I be as one who veils herself by the flocks of your companions?

"One who veils herself." What does that mean? A veil is a symbol of shame. You're covering your face so no one can see you. Prostitutes back in those days wore veils over their faces because they didn't want anyone to see them in the profession they were in. So, she's saying to the king, "I can't show my face to the flock. Look at me... I'm a mess... they'll reject me. I'm messed up, and I've let you down. This is too painful. I can't face the flock and I can't face you, so I'm wearing a veil." This is the place that the enemy ultimately wants to take you, every single time... "I'm not worthy of your love." That's where it's all leading to. It's all leading to accusing God of not loving you, or accusing you of not being worthy enough of His love. Then we start believing those lies, and that's a sad, dangerous place to be. That's where this Shulamite woman is as she questions the king.

Worthiness is based on worth. If you're judging your worth before God based on your actions, behaviors and deeds then it's easy to come to the conclusion that you're not worthy. But your true worth in God's eyes is the price He paid for you, and you can't put a price tag on the blood of Jesus and His sacrifice. So, you can't come before God and say, "I'm not worthy of Your love, because I was bad today." He says, "I knew that two thousand years ago. This doesn't surprise me what you're doing today. I knew about it two thousand years ago, and I made a way for you to be worthy through my Son's precious blood."

So, when the enemy starts telling you, "You're not worthy," you can reply, "You know, you're right. I will never be worthy of what God did for me. Never! But I receive what He did, and that's what makes me worthy!"

So, the Shulamite woman is hiding behind her veil. She hates having to hide behind it, though. Nobody likes having to hide, but that's the first thing the enemy does to us when we've done wrong... he tries to make us ashamed... he tries to isolate us. "I can't go back to church. I can't be seen in public. People are going to reject me. Everybody knows what an awful person I am now." Those are a bunch of lies straight from the enemy.

Another group of people who wore veils in the Bible, besides prostitutes, was lepers. They carried an incurable disease and it forced them to live outside the camp. It forced them to be shunned and isolated. They wore a veil to hide their diseased faces. Similarly, this Shulamite woman felt shunned and isolated. She felt like an outcast as she hid her face behind the veil.

What happens to a person when they're isolated? I find myself frequently warning the Body of Christ about the dangers of isolation. You see, when a person leaves the Body of Christ they are opening themselves up to an attack, because they become an isolated target. There's protection in numbers. When a sheep leaves the flock they become open to a wolf's attack. It's no different with us humans. We have an enemy that wants to isolate us from God's other sheep so he can attack us more easily. When Jesus was here on Earth He sent His disciples to "the lost sheep of Israel." I love that! He said, "Go, leave the ninety-nine and find the one." He knew that those who had left the sheepfold were vulnerable to attack. He wanted them to be brought back to the safety of the fold. He also commanded His disciples, "Cleanse the lepers." This was part of the heart of His mission, and still is today. He wants to minister to those who are the outcasts of society. He wants to find the sheep who have left the fold. He wants everyone to find their place in Him.

FOLLOW THE FOOTSTEPS OF THE FLOCK

The Shulamite woman was in this place of desperation. She wants to be with him, to be refreshed and to find rest, but isn't sure if she has found favor in his eyes. The king responds to her sweetly and tenderly. He doesn't judge her or condemn her for feeling the way she does. He replies:

Song of Solomon 1:8 (NKJV)
If you do not know, O fairest among women, follow in the footsteps of the flock, and feed your little goats beside the shepherds' tents.

He's telling her, "If you need to be fed, if you need to rest, if you want to find me, follow the flock that knows where I am… follow those who know me… follow them, and you'll find me." Some people say, "I don't like church." "I don't like to be with Christians." (Here's a big one I hear quite often) "I can serve God on my own. I don't have to go to church. I can have church in my own house by myself." These people are setting themselves up for attack! They are deceived. There's a really good reason why the scripture says, "Don't forsake the assembling of yourselves together." We need the support and strength of others who are in the Body of Christ. There is protection from our enemy in the sheepfold. So, He's telling her, "If you can't find me, follow the footsteps of the flock." What does that mean? It means that we should look at the history of all those who have gone before us. Follow the path of those who have successfully followed the Lord and made it all the way. Follow them.

The Apostle Paul said, "Follow me, as I follow Christ." Follow those that you know have a close walk with the Lord. If you need to get close to Him, get next to somebody who is already close to Him and it won't be long before you're in His presence. Follow those that you know are passionately in love with Jesus. Don't hang around with people who are backslidden. Don't hang around people who don't know the Lord. You won't get in God's presence that way. Follow the footsteps of the flock.

Follow the life of Billy Graham. He was a man that stayed faithful in service to the Lord for decades and led millions of people to

Finding Your Place at the King's Table

the Lord. Follow the life of Corrie ten Boom. She went through hell on earth in Nazi Germany prison camps. She came through all of her struggles and adversity loving Jesus. She's a beautiful example of God's power to deliver us through the worst of life's circumstances. Follow the footsteps of this woman of God and you'll find God, and you'll find the place where He feeds His flocks.

If following the lives of Billy Graham and Corrie ten Boom seems too daunting, I'll give you a less famous example to follow... the life of Judi Valencia. You see, years and years ago when I was going through my own personal hell after my husband's affair, I remember a prayer that I lifted up to the Lord. I was in my bedroom. I was on my knees, crying my eyes out because I had lost everything. I prayed, "Lord, Make me Your poster child of what You can do with a destroyed life. When they look at this face, let them say, 'If God can do it for her, He can do it for me.'" Follow those who have made it through. Follow those who have something to say that's been validated. I didn't have a nervous breakdown. I didn't backslide. I didn't turn my back on God. I know God to be faithful. I know God always keeps His Word. He said He would never leave me or forsake me. He said He'd take everything that Satan threw at me and turn it around someday. Although I'd never wish what happened to me upon my worst enemy, still I wouldn't trade it for anything, because during all my trials God brought me to a new place in Him. Follow the footsteps of those who have gone before you and have made it through.

Another testimony of someone who has gone through great adversity and made it through is my sister. She has lost two daughters to cancer. Both died in their thirtieth year of age. I just look at her sometimes and ask, "How can you do this? How can you make it through this?" Of course, I know the answer... God is her strength. She's a pillar of strength. I've told her on many occasions, "You are so strong," and she replies, every time, "It's not me." She knows where her strength comes from.

So, here this Shulamite woman is asking, "Where do you feed your flock, and where do you make it rest?" The king replies, "Follow in the footsteps of the flock." Follow in the footsteps of those who have a strength that comes from God alone. Isaiah 40:11 says that, "He will feed His flock like a shepherd...." Isn't that beautiful? He has promised to feed us. He says that He'll even, "carry the little ones in His arm, in His bosom and gently lead them."

Now, the king not only told her where he feeds his flock, he also told her where the little goats feed. He said, "Feed your little goats beside the shepherds' tents." This reference to "little goats" is a reference to little children, I believe. Yes, God cares about the little ones in our lives. That's so important to remember, especially for stay-at-home mothers who are sometimes separated from those times of intimacy with the Lord because of the demanding task of raising young children. God gives women special grace during that season in their lives.

THE GOOD SHEPHERD

The word "feed" here, from "where do you *feed* your flock," is the Hebrew word Ra'ah. It means "to shepherd, to tend, to pasture." He wants to feed every one of us. There are times in our lives that we get pulled away from His presence, when we're not in His Word, not in fellowship with other believers, and we get so hungry and dry. It's an unfortunate truth that even though God often fills us up with His presence and anointing, we tend to leak... we start draining. We go to church and ask God to fill us up, and He does. Then we go out into the world in our everyday lives and "swoosh"... all that life and anointing gets sucked right out of us. We need to be fed. We need to be replenished often. That word "feed" is used one hundred and seventy times in the Old Testament. God wants to feed us and replenish us so we can take our place in this world and be strong for Him.

The Bible talks about David feeding his flock when he was a young boy. When he became an adult he was crowned and anointed as King over Israel. He became the *shepherd* of Israel. All of the experiences he had leading his flock of sheep during his youth was preparing him for leading the sheepfold of Israel when he became king. So, what you're doing right now is preparing you for greater things in the future. David started out tending a small flock of sheep, but he ended up shepherding God's entire flock of Israel. Let this serve as encouragement to you if you're serving in ministry to infants and children today... you may be shepherding the whole flock tomorrow.

Now, remember, David wrote Psalm 23. I want you to see a connection here. Since David had spent many years of his youth feeding his flock and tending to them, he understood what the flock needed. When he became shepherd over God's people, he clued us into the secret of his success when he wrote, "The Lord is my Shepherd." He was saying, "You may have me as your shepherd, but I have a Shepherd too, and He knows exactly what I need. And, because He knows what I need, I SHALL NOT WANT. I shall not lack for any good thing because my Shepherd takes care of me. He makes me lie down in green pastures."

The Shulamite woman asked, "Where do you feed your flock? Where do you make it rest at noon?" David answered that question in Psalm 23... "He leads me beside still waters." That's a place of refreshing and rest. "He restores my soul." Do you need your soul restored? My Shepherd restores my soul. What is the soul? It is our mind, will, and emotions. It's that part of us that gets beat up all week long. He's the one who restores our soul. Let's take a moment to remind ourselves of all the benefits of having the Lord as our Shepherd.

Psalm 23:3-5 (NKJV)
3 He restores my soul; He leads me in the paths of righteousness for His name's sake.

4 Yea, though I walk through the valley of the shadow of death, I will fear no evil; for You are with me; Your rod and Your staff, they comfort me.
5 You prepare a table before me in the presence of my enemies; You anoint my head with oil; my cup runs over.

If you think about it, Psalm 23 could be your whole salvation story. Your whole walk with the Lord is wrapped up in that one little Psalm when you know Jesus as your Shepherd. He leads you. He vindicates you. He heals you. He provides for you. He protects you. It's all right there in Psalm 23.

Now, there are several Messianic prophecies about Jesus being a Shepherd. I'm going to share a couple of them with you and then tie them together.

Ezekiel 34:23 (NKJV)
I will establish one shepherd over them, and he shall feed them.... He shall feed them and be their shepherd.

Micah 5:4 (NKJV)
And He shall stand and feed His flock in the strength of the Lord.

These are prophecies referring to the ministry of Jesus, written hundreds of years before His earthly ministry. Jesus has the heart of a shepherd. These prophecies tell us that Jesus will do two things as our Shepherd: 1) He will feed the sheep, and 2) He will give strength to the sheep. Now let's look again at the wording of Song of Solomon 1:7-8.

Song of Solomon 1:7 (NKJV)
Tell me, O you whom I love, where you feed your flock, where you make it rest at noon.

She is saying she needs to be fed, and she needs the strength that comes from finding rest. Food and rest. That's what she's needing, and that's what the prophecies tell us the Messiah will bring to the flock of God. Once again we are being reminded that even though this is a true story in history between King Solomon and the Shulamite woman, there is also a prophetic undertone in these passages foretelling of the Good Shepherd and His earthly ministry to the flock of God.

Song of Solomon 1:8 (NKJV)
If you do not know, O fairest among women, follow in the footsteps of the flock, and feed your little goats beside the shepherds' tents.

Take note that Solomon calls her "O fairest among women." Another translation says "most lovely." Even in your weakness, when you are at your worst, the Good Shepherd calls you lovely. He sees you as beautiful. He calls you His beloved.

The church has got to come into this identity of the loving King and Shepherd. If we don't understand that this is how He sees us, we will run *from* Him instead of *to* Him. He tells her to follow the footsteps of those who have gone before. And, then He tells her to feed the little ones. This can have two meanings. 1) The little ones are those children entrusted to the care of the church, and 2) the little ones are baby Christians who are coming into the kingdom of God. He told her to keep them close to the Shepherd's tent. We have a responsibility to the physically young and the spiritually young to protect them by leading them to the Good Shepherd... encouraging them to remain in a close relationship with Him.

YOU'RE HIS WARHORSE

Now, let's take a look at verses 9 and 10. Solomon is looking at this woman who is throwing her heart on the altar, so to speak, and she's saying, "I need your help. I surrender. I know where to go for my help." He looks at her with love. He tells her she is lovely. Then he says to her:

Song of Solomon 1:9-10 (NKJV)
9 I have compared you, my love, to my filly among Pharaoh's chariots.
10 Your cheeks are lovely with ornaments, your neck with chains of gold.

What is he talking about? He's saying, "You are my love and you remind me of a warhorse that is decorated for battle. Isn't that powerful! You might see yourself as broken down and burnt out because of the darkness of your sin, but He sees you as beautiful. He sees you as a decorated warhorse, full of strength, dignity and royalty. He doesn't see you as you see yourself.

Song of Solomon 1:11 (NKJV)
We will make you ornaments of gold with studs of silver.

Verse 11 is the reaction of the daughters of Jerusalem to what he said to her. Remember, you have spectators in your life who are watching everything you do. They're just waiting for one little slip-up, so they can say, "See. You think you're so holy! You think you're a Christian. Ha!" The Bible says the devil is the accuser of the brethren. He'll accuse you through the voices of others who are watching you. But, you've got somebody in your life who sees the darkness, who sees the slip-ups, who sees the past wrongs, yet still says, "You are dark, but you are lovely. You're my warhorse decorated for battle. You are royalty!" Oh! You've got to know who you are. You've got to know so these spectators who are watching can catch on... so they can see this beautiful relationship you have with your Lord. Here, in verse 11, the daughters of Jerusalem are seeing this love affair unfold and they say, "We want to make ornaments of gold for you."

They're saying to one another, "There must be something to this. The king is promoting her. She's being recognized by the king. If the king sees that kind of worth and value in her then we should do the same. Let's decorate her. Let's add to the décor. Let's put expensive accessories on her." You see, the first thing that happens when you start coming into who you are is some of those old garments get stripped away so the royal garments can be put on in their place. He wants you to have garments of splendor and beauty, so He starts clothing you, saying, "This is who you are. This is your identity. Now we're going to dress you like a queen. We're going to dress you like a warhorse." Isn't that good! When you get back to where you belong in the Lord, to the person He's called you to be, He's going to clothe you in royalty. He's going to put you on display as a decorated warhorse. He's not seeing you as simply a beautiful Bride, with glitter and frills. No! He's seeing you as a Warrior Bride!

SITTING AT THE KING'S TABLE

Song of Solomon 1:12-14 (NKJV)
12 While the king is at his table, my spikenard sends forth its fragrance.
13 A bundle of myrrh is my beloved to me, that lies all night between my breasts.
14 My beloved is to me a cluster of henna blooms in the vineyards of En Gedi.

Now, this portion of scripture might cause some people to stumble, but let me break this down for you because it's one of my favorite sections of Song of Solomon. While sitting at the table with the king, this Shulamite woman is now beginning to see him in all his majesty. She had nothing to offer except for a life of shame, guilt, and darkness, yet she's sitting at the king's table. She's gazing upon his royalty and majesty and is overwhelmed by what she sees. Have you ever gotten just the smallest glimpse of Jesus? Have you ever seen Him in all of His majesty and authority? If you have, you know that it changes you. You begin to understand why the cherubim who surround His throne continually cry out, "Holy, Holy, Holy is the Lord God Almighty." When you get a glimpse of Him you can't help but join the angel chorus. "Holy, Holy, Holy!" Those angels can't say anything else!

So, this woman is sitting at the king's table. She doesn't deserve to be there, but the king invited her there because he loves her. She asked the king, "Where do you feed your flock" and he says, "Come have a seat at my table." Look at Song of Solomon 2:4 for a moment.

Song of Solomon 2:4 (NKJV)
He brought me to the banqueting house, and his banner over me was love.

Love brought you to that table! Psalms 23:5 says, "You prepare a table before me in the presence of my enemies." That's the king's table. Your enemies are watching as Jesus pulls the chair out and says, "Sit at my table." Those who said, "You'll never amount to anything," those who said, "You'll never be able to overcome your past," they're watching you sit down at the king's table and they're realizing they should have never mocked you. You're eating food made for a king, dressed in royal attire.

Now, in the first part of that next verse, she's telling what "my beloved is to me." He's already told her what she is to him. He's told her that she's lovely, and that she's like a decorated warhorse. She's starting to see herself the way he sees her. She's starting to put some pieces together. In response, she says what her beloved is to her. "My beloved is to me a pouch of myrrh." Now that might not make sense to us because myrrh is not something we're familiar with too much here in Western civilization. You see, myrrh is a spice that's used quite frequently in the Middle East, and it was mostly used by very wealthy people. It was a burial spice and it was very, very expensive. It smells very sweet, but it's very bitter to taste.

She's beginning to realize the very expensive, extravagant price that the King paid for her. It was so sweet to her, but so bitter to Him. He paid the price for it. The myrrh represents Christ's death on the cross, and she says, "I remember all night long upon my heart what He did for me. That myrrh stays between my breasts, upon my heart, all the time, day and night." Again, as I've mentioned earlier, the mention of "breasts" here is not to be thought of in a sexual way. This is not a sex manual, it's a love affair. She's saying, "I remember what you did for me. It's permeating my heart."

THE BLOOD-BOUGHT BRIDE

Then she says, "My beloved is to me a cluster of henna blooms in the vineyards of En Gedi." First of all, henna blooms grew alongside the Dead Sea, and these vineyards carried the most beautiful fragrance throughout Israel. Henna blooms were used in wedding ceremonies. They would take the blooms, which were red, and stain the brides hands with it. This marked her for the ceremony and identified her as the bride. When she says, "My beloved is to me a cluster of henna blooms," she's saying, "I am marked as his bride. What he did is in my heart, and it permeates my being, and now I am marked as his bride." The red also symbolizes that she is marked with the blood of the Lamb. That red stain upon her skin is a reminder of the price that was paid for her… the price of the dowry that Jesus paid to claim her as His own. You see, we are to be stained in the blood of the Lamb. We are to be marked as His Bride and what He did for us is supposed to permeate our hearts.

DOVE'S EYES

Now that she has told him what he is to her, he responds to her with:

Song of Solomon 1:15 (NKJV)
Behold, you are fair, my love! Behold, you are fair! You have dove's eyes.

"You are fair" means "You are beautiful." And, he doesn't just say it once... he says it twice, to make sure that she really gets it. She poured out the fragrance of spikenard at his table. She's becoming a sweet smell to him. She's becoming a beautiful fragrance. He's seeing the transformation not only in her outward beauty but also in her inward beauty. So, he says, "You are beautiful." He says it even louder the second time, "You are so beautiful my love!" "*My love*"... he's declaring his ownership of her by calling her "*My* love." He's letting everyone know the way he feels about her. I find oftentimes in prophetic ministry that God will single a person out and have them stand up so the prophet can speak words of love from the Father to that person for all to hear. He wants others to know the way He feels about that person. He doesn't keep it private.

He says, "You have dove's eyes." Why would he say that? Something interesting about doves eyes is that they don't have peripheral vision. They cannot see anything except for what is directly in front of them. They cannot see to the right or to the left. They only see what's right in front of them. They can only focus on one thing at a time. Something else that's interesting about doves is that they mate for life. If one of the pair dies, the other will never re-mate.

I saw this first hand one time, right in my backyard. We have a bird feeder right outside my kitchen window and I watched two pairs of doves sitting on a fence, waiting to go to the bird feeder. While they were sitting there a huge hawk swooped down and took one of the four. This was two years ago. Now, for the past two years there have been 3 doves visiting my feeder, because the one who lost its mate never re-mated. It's sad to think about, but it shows the faithfulness displayed in this gentle bird. The king said, "You have dove's eyes."

God wants to bring us into a relationship where He's not worried about losing us. He says, "I want you to have eyes only for Me. I want you to have "single vision." Isn't that good! And, her response to him is:

Song of Solomon 1:16 (NKJV)
Behold, you are handsome, my beloved! Yes, pleasant! Also our bed is green.

A PLACE OF INTIMACY

She calls him "handsome." Do you know there's a verse in Proverbs that says that kindness makes a man handsome? My husband, John, is the most handsome man on this planet according to that scripture. His kindness makes him incredibly handsome. She looks at him and calls him "handsome" as she revels in the kindness of the king. Romans 2:4 tells us that the kindness of the Lord leads us to repentance.

Then she says, "Our bed is green." Another translation says "verdant" instead of "green." When your bed is green, what does that mean? The bed symbolizes a place of intimacy. The color green represents life. When something is green it is alive, living, active and vibrant. "Our bed is green," means that there is living intimacy in this relationship. I hate to say it, but many Christians live in a dead bed… there's no intimacy in their relationship with the Lord. God wants you to experience intimacy with Him.

Song of Solomon 1:17 (NKJV)
The beams of our houses are cedar….

Cedar is a very strong wood that can not be eaten up by worms.

Song of Solomon 1:17 (NKJV)
… and our rafters of fir.

Rafters were the support beams that held up the house, and they were built using red fir trees. *Red* fir covered their home. So she's saying, "Our home is covered with the blood. It cannot be eaten by worms. It cannot be destroyed. Our bed is green and our intimacy is alive and glorious.

Now, think about it. Just seven verses earlier she was on the outside looking in. But, now she's in this intimate place, inside the house, in the king's chamber, in an intimate relationship with the king. It's such a beautiful story of redemption!

God doesn't want any of us to be "on the outside looking in." He wants to bring us to His banqueting table. He wants us to be in His house. When you got to church on Sunday morning you didn't bring yourself... He brought you there. He made a way. He's your Shepherd. This poor shepherd girl represents every one of us. At one time or another we've all been in a mess in our lives. It's called "being a human." No one is exempt from imperfections. It's just part of living on this planet, right? But, God wants to take you from that place of religion where you think you've got to be good enough, or worthy enough to receive His blessing, to a place where you can come and sit down at the king's table. He'll pull the chair out for you, He'll pull off your old garments and have you put on beautiful, new royal garments. Nobody deserves that kind of treatment. Nobody is worthy of it, but He does it anyway, because He is so kind and loving. It's like a fairy tale that's too good to be true. But it is true!

This is what every heart is looking for. Right now, there's a woman at a bar down the road who is sitting there thinking, "Will somebody please just love me for who I am. Somebody please be that knight in shining armor I've dreamed about." There's a man sitting there wishing that he could find that special woman he's been looking for all his life. All of those hopes and dreams for true intimacy are fulfilled in God. He loves you deeply and completely. You don't have to do anything to deserve His love and acceptance. He's not mad at you. Religion tells you He's mad at you, but He's not an angry God... He is LOVE. When we feel like we can't come to Him it's because something is wrong in the way we're thinking. Our mind is saying "This is too good to be true." But, if we'll listen to our hearts, where God is speaking to us, we can hear Him say, "Come, take a seat at my table."

CHAPTER 5
WINTER IS PAST!

We are going to start off chapter 5 by looking at Song of Solomon 2:1-13. I will preface each passage by telling you who is doing the talking. Verse 1 is the Shulamite woman speaking.

Song of Solomon 2:1 (NKJV)
I am the rose of Sharon, and the lily of the valleys.

King Solomon replies to her in verse 2.

Song of Solomon 2:2 (NKJV)
Like a lily among thorns, so is my love among the daughters.

She responds to his words of love with her own words of love and affection for him.

Song of Solomon 2:3 (NKJV)
Like an apple tree among the trees of the woods, so is my beloved among the sons. I sat down in his shade with great delight, and his fruit was sweet to my taste.

In verses 4-6, she's speaking to the daughters of Jerusalem, and also to the king.

Song of Solomon 2:4-7 (NKJV)
4 He brought me to the banqueting house, and his banner over me was love. (Speaking to the daughters of Jerusalem)
5 Sustain me with cakes of raisins, refresh me with apples, for I am lovesick. (Speaking to the king)
6 His left hand is under my head, and his right hand embraces me. (Speaking again to the daughters of Jerusalem)

The king responds with a word of admonition to the daughters of Jerusalem:

Song of Solomon 2:7 (NKJV)
7 I charge you, O daughters of Jerusalem, by the gazelles or by the does of the field, do not stir up nor awaken love until it pleases.

You can't beat somebody over the head with a Bible, hoping that will reach them for God's kingdom. No! You can't awaken love until it pleases. They've got to get that revelation of His love for themselves. They've got to come to an understanding of who He is and how much He loves them as an individual. This is one of my favorite things to teach, by the way. You see, we've tried to force a relationship with the Lord on people, but this shows us plainly that there is a proper time and place when love is awakened, and we need to be sensitive to that.

Next, the Shulamite is going to be speaking:

Song of Solomon 2:8-13 (NKJV)
8 The voice of my beloved! Behold, he comes leaping upon the mountains, skipping upon the hills.
9 My beloved is like a gazelle or a young stag. Behold, he stands behind our wall; he is looking through the windows, gazing through the lattice.
10 My beloved spoke, and said to me: "Rise up, my love, my fair one, and come away.
11 For lo, the winter is past...

Just a footnote here. I preached this message at my home church recently, and it just so happened that it was the very first Sunday of spring... winter had officially passed. I had not planned it intentionally, so it was obvious that the timing was from the Holy Spirit. I love it when He gives us little kisses like that!

Song of Solomon 2:11-13 (NKJV)
11 For lo, the winter is past, the rain is over and gone.
12 The flowers appear on the earth; the time of singing has come, and the voice of the turtledove is heard in our land.
13 The fig tree puts forth her green figs, and the vines with the tender grapes give a good smell. Rise up, my love, my fair one, and come away!

I get goosebumps reading that! It's so romantic. Such a beautiful picture of what being in love feels like. Do you remember the first time you met your first love, or the one you were to marry, and you just felt something deep down inside of you that was unexplainable? Love was fresh and so incredibly real to you. I remember feeling that way when I first met my husband, John. I went into panic mode. I prayed to the Lord, "If this isn't you God, get rid of it now, 'cause I'm feeling something!" That's what's going on in this conversation between the Shulamite woman and the king. There is a passion involved... there is a fire! These two people are crazy in love with one another. That's what you're hearing in this conversation in Song of Solomon chapter 2. But, remember, this is symbolic of our own love relationship with the Lord as His Bride. This is Him romancing us, and us responding to His love with words of praise and affection. This is the "too good to be true" fairy tale that really is true! This is a dream come true.

YOU'VE COME A LONG WAY

If we go back to the beginning of Song of Solomon, we're reminded of how far the Shulamite woman has come in this relationship. At first we saw her simply as a poor peasant girl who had nothing to bring to the king. She had nothing to offer him at all. She was a simple, lowly shepherdess who ended up working in the vineyards of her brothers. Her skin had gotten weathered and dark from working in the heat of the day. She was probably stained on her fingers from the grapes. Appearance-wise, she was a mess. But, out of all the women that Solomon had (and he had a *lot* of women), he chose her. She had said, "Don't look me. I'm dark. I'm stained. I'm worn out. I'm exhausted." But, he replied, "You may be dark, but you are lovely." He lovingly wooed her to himself.

Do you know that God has been wooing you? A more modern term to use would be *allure*. He is *alluring* you. He has been baiting you with His love. You've had all of these walls and insecurities that you've built up in an attempt to keep others out. You've not wanted anyone to get too close to you because they might see into you. Remember, the word *intimacy* is "in-to-me-see." You haven't wanted anyone to get in there to see what's inside of you. But, He's been luring you by His love and He's been getting closer and closer. He's been saying to you, "Come closer. Come closer to me."

THE ROSE OF SHARON

Chapter 2 begins with the Shulamite woman explaining how she sees herself. "I am the rose of Sharon, a lily of the valley." The rose of Sharon in Israel is not like the American rose of Sharon which grows really tall and out of control. In Israel, the rose of Sharon is very small and insignificant, and grows very close to the ground. So she is saying, "I am very lowly and insignificant. This is how I see myself."

Now, Sharon is a geographical location within Israel. It is near the coastal plain. Sharon is a place with very rich, fertile soil. That's why this particular rose grows so well there. So, taking all of this symbolism into consideration, we see that the Shulamite woman is saying, "I am lowly and insignificant, but I've been put in a very rich place. I'm being nourished in this place so I can become more than what I am."

THE LILY OF THE VALLEY

She goes on to say, "I am the lily of the valley." She continues describing herself poetically as a blooming plant. In Israel, the lily of the valley is a tall plant, but it has a very weak stem. The flower droops over the stem. The Shulamite woman is acknowledging her weakness before her king. She's saying, "I am lowly and insignificant, and very weak, yet, somehow this king has put me in a place of nourishment. Even in the midst of my dark valley, I bloom."

The king responds to her by saying, "Like a lily among thorns, is my love among the young women." He doesn't even address what she said about the rose of Sharon. He ignores that completely. In so doing, he is saying, "I don't see you as small, lowly and insignificant. Instead, you are a lily among the thorns in my eyes. You stand out among all the rest to me. I can't miss your beauty. Even in your weakness I find you lovely."

Lilies are symbolic of purity. He tells her she stands out like a lily among thorns. Thorns are very symbolic throughout the scriptures. Do you remember when Jesus talked about the seeds that grew among the thorns in the parable of the sower? The thorns choked out the good seeds that were planted. I had a lilac plant growing in my yard and it was beautiful, but a thorn bush grew up and choked that beautiful plant. Thorns are destructive, and even dangerous. You know this if you've ever been pricked by a thorn bush. They can be very painful. So, the king tells her she is like a pure lily growing in the midst of a dark and cruel world, filled with thorns. Thorns that want to choke the life out of her. Somehow, though, she has been resilient and has risen above the thorns. In the midst of her trouble and danger, the king saw her as a beautiful, tall lily.

The word "lily" is used 15 times in the Bible. Eight of those times is found in the Song of Solomon. Something very interesting and profound about the lily is that it can have up to 50 bulbs underneath it. That made it the most productive plant in all of Israel. Now, this is why we should never judge other people, especially by what we see on the surface. God sees what's underneath. He sees what's hidden inside a person. He sees the gifts and the talents. He sees all that He's placed deep down in the roots of who a person is. He knows what you and I were meant to be, even if it hasn't manifested beyond the surface yet. Only God can see the true heart of a person.

You may be going through a valley right now, but God knows what He's placed inside of you, and He's going to watch you excel and bloom in the valley. When everyone else said you wouldn't make it, God said, "You're better than you know! You will overcome! You're a lily of the valley!"

There's one other important fact about the lily of the valley. They're watered by the dew of the ground. Hosea 14:5 says, "*I will be like the dew to Israel.*" The morning dew brings refreshing and nourishment to the lily of the valley. Likewise, the refreshing dew of God revitalizes and nourishes us as we grow in Him.

Song of Solomon 2:2 (NKJV)
Like a lily among thorns, so is my love among the daughters.

Take note of this proclamation from the lips of the king: "So is my love among the daughters." He is saying, "You are my love, you are my favorite, and you are beautiful. You stand out in the crowd and you move my heart." Those are words we need to hear as the Lord's beloved. Sure, we love to shower Him with praise and adoration, and tell Him how much we love Him. But, do you realize that He wants to do the same for us? He wants to shower His love and affection upon us. He wants to tell us how much He loves us. That's why I love worship songs that express God's love for us as well as our love for Him. It is a mutually beneficial relationship that we're in. You see, I don't just love *His* presence... He loves *mine*! A divine exchange takes place in a true worship service. It's not all just a one-way conversation. I get goosebumps sometimes when I hear the Holy Spirit speak to me with God's words of love and affection for me.

THE APPLES OF GOD'S WORD

Song of Solomon 2:3 (NKJV)
Like an apple tree among the trees of the woods, so is my beloved among the sons. I sat down in his shade with great delight, and his fruit was sweet to my taste.

Now, verse 3 is the Shulamite woman responding back to the king after he tells her that she stands out above all the rest like a lily among the thorns. Notice that she compares her love to an apple tree here. Apples are special to me. It seems like everywhere I turn there's some reference to apples in my life. As a matter of fact, I live on a street called Apple Court. So, I love Bible references to apples. In this verse, she is saying that her lover stands out from all the rest like an apple tree in the middle of a forest full of other trees. The apple tree's blossoms are gorgeous and very fragrant, and the fruit from the apple tree is sweet and delicious.

Throughout the Bible, God uses apples to describe His Word. If we skip ahead in Song of Solomon to chapter 8 verse 5 we read:

Song of Solomon 8:5 (NKJV)
I awakened you under the apple tree. There your mother brought you forth; there she who bore you brought you forth.

When you see the word "mother" in Song of Solomon it is referring to the church. So, what the king is saying is, "I awakened you under the apple tree, where you first heard my words in the church, when you got born again. My words were apples for your nourishment." Proverbs 25:11 adds further confirmation to this idea.

Proverbs 25:11 (NKJV)
A word fitly spoken is like apples of gold in settings of silver.

God says, "My Word is gold to you. My Word awakened you when you came to My House (the church)."

So, she says to him, "You're an apple tree to me." By the way, there's not just one apple on an apple tree. There are dozens and hundreds of them. And, the seed inside each apple will produce more trees filled with more apples. God's Words of promise and encouragement are abundant in our lives and bring nourishment to us!

I want to show you Song of Solomon 8:5 in The Passion Translation because I love the way it's stated:

Song of Solomon 8:5 (TPT)
Who is this one? Look at her now! She arises out of her desert, clinging to her beloved. When I awakened you under the apple tree, as you were feasting upon me, I awakened your innermost being with the travail of birth as you longed for more of me.

Oh! Something in you was crying out. Something in you was longing and aching for more. He allured you. He pulled you into the wilderness. He called you to Himself and started feeding you apples. He started feeding you with apples from His tree. These apples were the promises found in His Word. He started giving you juicy, sweet apples… nuggets of truth that nourished your spirit.

Psalm 34:8 (NKJV)
Oh, taste and see that the Lord is good!

Taste that apple. When you taste the fruit from God's tree you can taste and see that the Lord is good. The enemy had Eve bite into fruit that wasn't from God's tree. It was counterfeit. He's still using the same counterfeit fruit in this world today, trying to lure people away from the goodness of God. But, when we taste that apple from God's tree, and experience the good promises from His Word, something awakens inside of us. Something comes alive. When we taste the Word of God our soul is refreshed and it gives birth to our spirit man... it makes our spirit man come alive.

Now, I mentioned earlier that it seems everywhere I turn I'm seeing prophetic references to apples in my life. For instance, we recently bought a king-size box spring and mattress at one store and a frame for the bed at another store. When we got the bed all put together, it was too high off the ground for me to get into it. So, I needed bed steps. Well, everywhere I looked online they were well over $100, and I was thinking that was way too expensive. My husband John walked into a store, and I guess he must have been led by the Spirit of God, because he found just what we needed at a very reasonable price. When I took a look at the steps I noticed that there were apples on them. Do you see the symbolism? The steps to the bridal chamber were prophetically decorated with the fruit of God's Word.

I'd like to relate one more story, as it concerns apples, to show you the prophetic symbolism they hold in my life. A few years ago I had a dream that I was in a very huge building. It was the size of a football stadium. Inside this building there were prison cells everywhere. In those prison cells there were dark-skinned people; black, brown, light brown. They were all behind these bars. The Lord showed me that these prison cells were prophetically symbolic of an inner-city area that we, as a church, were wanting to reach out to with the gospel. In the dream, I carried a brown paper bag filled with fresh apples. John, my husband, was also with me and he had a bag of apples as well. We went throughout that whole building handing fresh apples to everyone in the cells.

Now, the apples, of course, were symbolic of God's Word. We were sharing God's Word with those prisoners in that poverty-stricken area. Whenever I would run out of apples, John would hand me another bag so I could continue handing them out without stopping. Well, in one of the cells there was a gentleman standing there with one hand out to receive an apple, but his other hand was in his pocket. He motioned for me to come over to him as he said, "Come here." When I went over to give him an apple, he took my hand, turned it over, pulled a fig out of his pocket and placed it into my hand. The Lord spoke to my heart, "You reach the poor, and I'll reach the Jews." He said, "You keep going into that poverty-stricken area; you keep feeding them, and loving them, and bringing them the Word of God, and I will give you the Jews."

So, again, apples are very prophetic and symbolic. They represent the Word of God and the promises of God. Taste and see that the Lord is good! He is good!

GOD'S BANQUETING HOUSE

Song of Solomon 2:4 (NKJV)
He brought me to the banqueting house, and his banner over me was love.

He brought me... He brought you. You didn't bring yourself. He brought you. You didn't have anything to do with it. You were out in the world doing your own thing. You were doing whatever made you happy. And He said, "Wait a minute. Eat this apple. Eat this apple and come to my table. I've got a feast for you. I have a banquet for you."

Now notice, as we look back to chapter 1 verse 4, the king brought her first into his chambers. The first thing God does is He woos you into His chambers. That's your awakening. That's your salvation experience. But then, the romance continues as the king takes her to the table where he has a feast prepared. God is showing you that He has more for you. It doesn't stop at salvation. He says, "I've got a feast for you that you don't know about. It's not just salvation that I offer you. There's a whole banqueting table here for you!" One translation says "banqueting hall." It's not just a table, because a table can't hold it all. The actual, literal translation for banqueting table is "house of wine." We're leaving the bridal chamber and going to the house of wine. He's saying, "Now that I have awakened you through salvation, and fed you with the apples of My Word, I'm bringing you to the next level of your salvation experience into the house of wine, where I'm going to fill you with My Holy Spirit! I'm not just interested in *saving* you... I want to *fill* you!"

"THE HOUSE OF WINE"

In the "house of wine," the king introduced his beloved to the source of her joy. Do you remember what Peter told the on-lookers on the Day of Pentecost when the disciples were baptized in the Holy Spirit and began to speak in other tongues? He said, "These men are not drunk as you suppose." They were immersed in the Holy Spirit. The house of wine is a place of celebration. It's a place of rejoicing in God's love. This King, who has everything, takes a woman who has nothing and brings her into the bridal chamber, and then opens up a whole hall filled with joy and celebration and love, and then baptizes her in His Spirit.

This is the place where He proposes to her, because the Bible also calls it "The Wedding Supper of the Lamb," or "The Wedding Feast of the Lamb." It is here that He seals her with His Spirit. Song of Solomon 8:6 says, "Place me like a seal over your heart." This seal over her heart signifies that she belongs to the King. All who belong to the Lord have this same seal upon their hearts. Ephesians 1:13 tells us, "You were sealed with the Holy Spirit of promise." God says, "You are mine. I just put my name on you." When a woman marries a man he gives her his name. I've been teaching people for years, "You are now Mrs. Jesus Christ." We've got to walk like that's who we are. We've got to act like that's who we are. When we walk into a place, we own it, because our husband gave it to us. This is what takes place when the King brings His bride into the banqueting hall.

HIS BANNER OVER ME IS LOVE

Song of Solomon 2:4 (NKJV)
... his banner over me was love.

Now, the Shulamite woman is getting the revelation and the download of what this king has done for her. He told her to come to the banqueting table, and she came. She didn't know all that awaited her. She discovers there's a new banner waving over her life. She once said of herself, "I'm dark. I'm stained. I'm lowly. I'm nothing." But, now she's saying, "His banner over me is love." Oh the difference God's love can make in a person's life! This new banner that waves over her defines her life now. The banner simply says "Love." There used to be depression, fear and oppression. There used to be slander and backbiting. All those old labels that once hung over her have now been replaced. She has a new label. She now realizes that she is fearfully and wonderfully made. The king's love for her has given her confidence in herself.

Back in Bible days banners were used by the military. The banner was symbolic of the authority of the kingdom whose image and name was on the banner. In the movie "Glory" with Matthew Broderick and Denzel Washington, there was a battle scene depicted near the end of the movie. Matthew Broderick's troops were about to storm a key fort that needed to be taken to ensure victory for the North in their battle against the South. It was basically a suicide mission. There was little hope that the troops would breach the walls of the fort. Broderick looked at his troops and saw the front man carrying the flag. The flag identified who they were fighting for and who they represented. Broderick looked at his men and challenged them with these words, "If this man should fall in battle who will pick up the flag?" Every time I hear that line I just get chills because it's so powerful.

Listen, if someone goes down in battle, don't stomp on them. Pick up the flag and wave it over them and run to the battle for them. As Christians, we don't beat one another up. We pick up the flag and press forward in battle. We help one another to ensure that the flag of love continues to wave over the Bride of Christ.

It's important to remember, also, that they didn't wave the banner when they were defeated in battle. They only waved it when they were victorious. It was a sign of victory. God says, "The battle has been won in your life. I wave the banner of love over you!"

When I first got saved I went to a Christian bookstore and bought a little button that said, "Jesus loved the devil out of me." I wanted people to see the love God had for me, so I wore that little button everywhere I went. I said, "God, you loved the devil out of me, and now I'm going to love the devil out of everybody I see!"

His banner over you is love, and He wants to raise that banner high over you for everyone to see. Many in the body of Christ aren't walking in that, unfortunately. They're not waving that banner of love victoriously for this world to see. Listen. There is a victory that's been purchased for us. The greatest act of violence ever perpetrated on this Earth was the crucifixion of Christ. But, it was also the greatest act of love this world has ever seen. So we need to proudly raise that banner over us and wave it, proclaiming God's victory in our lives.

THE SON, THE FATHER, THE HOLY SPIRIT

Let's recap the progression that has taken place between the king and the Shulamite woman. First, he took her to his chambers in chapter 1 verse 4. This represents our salvation experience where we come to know Jesus as Savior and Lord.

Then he took her to the table in chapter 1 verse 12. That table represents the Lord's Table... the place of communion and fellowship with the Father. This is where a lot of people have a problem in their relationship with God. They like the idea of calling Jesus their Savior and Lord, but they don't want to hear the word "Father" because it brings up bad feelings from their past. Perhaps they didn't have a good relationship with their earthly father so they need healing in that area. God starts to minister healing to that area of their life as they yield themselves at the communion table with Him.

Then He takes them on to the "house of wine" where they are introduced to the Holy Spirit. He doesn't want to leave us in the chambers where we only know Jesus through the salvation experience, but haven't gotten fully acquainted with the Father. Nor does He want to leave us at the table, communing with the Father, but neglecting a relationship with the Holy Spirit in the banqueting hall. We come to know Jesus as Lord, and God as our Father. We must also come to know the Holy Spirit as our best friend. We want a daily relationship with Him... the kind of relationship where we can say, "Holy Spirit, where did I leave my glasses?" to "Holy Spirit, show me how I need to pray for this person."

The Holy Spirit is my guide, my teacher, my counselor, my comforter. Jesus told his disciples, "It is to your advantage that I go away; for if I do not go away, the Helper will not come to you; but if I depart, I will send Him to you" (John 16:7). He was telling them that even though he was *with* them, he wasn't *in* them, but when He left, the Father would send the Holy Spirit so He could be *in* them.

I AM LOVESICK

Song of Solomon 2:5 (NKJV)
Sustain me with cakes of raisins, refresh me with apples, for I am lovesick.

At the banqueting hall, the Shulamite woman cries out, "Sustain me." I've cried out to the Lord with those same words of desperation before, and I'm sure you have also. "Lord, sustain me. Refresh me." She says, "Sustain me with cakes of raisins, refresh me with apples." Raisins are sweet and delicious and speak of the goodness of God, and the apples, as mentioned earlier, speak of the sweetness of God's Word. She's saying, "Lord, feed me with the sweetness of Your Word." Then, in heart-felt desperation, she cries out, "for I am lovesick." We sing a song at our church often that says, "I'm desperate for you." Oh, that we would have that kind of passion for the Lord always, longing for Him and His presence. We can all experience a measure of His presence in our own private devotional time with the Lord, but there's also something very special about the corporate anointing we experience when gathered together with the saints of God. There's nothing like the faith and fellowship of the saints coming together in that manifest, tangible Glory and Presence of God. It's a place where we cry out together as the Bride of Christ, "I'm desperate for you Lord! I'm lovesick!"

The Shulamite woman is saying, "I want more, and more. I can't get enough of you." She's been feeding at the king's table and it's created an unquenchable hunger in her. That's the neat thing about feasting at God's table. Even though He's fed you and you've gotten your fill of His goodness, you still want more... you're still hungry for more of Him. You can leave a Spirit-filled, anointed church service and within just a couple of hours all of that anointing seems to leak out of you. You get a phone call from your mother-in-law or you get in a little spat with your spouse, and, before you know it, the anointing just walked out the door. So you go to Jesus and cry out, "Lord, I'm desperate for you. I don't want to leave this place. I want to stay here in Your presence. Sustain me, Lord. Give me more of your love!"

GOD'S LEFT HAND AND RIGHT HAND

Song of Solomon 2:6 (NKJV)

His left hand is under my head, and his right hand embraces me.

Have you ever felt like you were going through the valley of the shadow of death? If you have, you've lived this verse. In the Bible, God's right hand is a sign of His mercy, and the left hand of God speaks of His justice. So, His right hand of mercy is embracing us, while His left hand of justice is holding our head up. Psalm 3:3 says, "But You, O Lord, are a shield for me, My glory and the One who lifts up my head." God is holding our head up. He's the glory and the lifter of our heads. So, don't hang your head. Hold your head up high, because He is going to bring justice where there's been injustice in your life.

GOD'S "DO NOT DISTURB" SIGN

Now, the king responds to the Shulamite woman in verse 7 with an admonition to the daughters of Jerusalem.

Song of Solomon 2:7 (NKJV)
I charge you, O daughters of Jerusalem, by the gazelles or by the does of the field, do not stir up nor awaken love until it pleases.

Remember, the daughters of Jerusalem are the onlookers. They're the naysayers, the backbiters, the religious crowd, the in-laws and the out-laws in your life that are watching you. The king says to them, "I am putting a 'do not disturb' sign over my bride. You're on the outside looking in. You have no idea what's going on between Me and My Bride. How dare you criticize her. How dare you say anything against My Bride. I am charging you right now... do not disturb My Bride! Touch not my anointed! My Bride is in a very strategic season. She's spending time with Me and learning about Me. Don't judge her by your religious opinions. Don't disrupt her. She's enjoying what I am giving her and doing for her. She's not fully mature yet, but she's getting there. Those bulbs beneath the ground, that you can't see, they're sending out roots. They're getting watered by My dew, and something's beginning to bud. Something's beginning to come forth. Spring is on its way!"

The king uses the phrase "by the gazelles or by the does of the field." Gazelles and does are very skittish animals. They are easily frightened. They jump at the slightest little noise or disruption. So, he's saying, "This is going to take some gentleness and sensitivity, so don't disturb or disrupt what I'm doing. Do not stir or awaken love until *it* pleases." Now, although he says "it" in reference to love, it is actually best translated as "she." "Don't disturb or awaken love until *she* pleases... until *she* is ready.

LET GOD IN!

The Shulamite woman responds to these words of the king in verse 8-9.

Song of Solomon 2:8-9 (NKJV)
8 The voice of my beloved! Behold, he comes leaping upon the mountains, skipping upon the hills.
9 My beloved is like a gazelle or a young stag. Behold, he stands behind our wall; he is looking through the windows, gazing through the lattice.

What are these mountains and hills being referred to in verse 8? The mountains are immovable obstacles in your life, and the hills are the struggles and problems that you have here on earth. He is leaping and skipping over them like a gazelle or young stag. You thought they were insurmountable obstacles in your life, but He skips right over them. Praise God!

Now, there is just one thing that can hinder the work that He's doing in our lives, and we see it in verse 9 where it says, "He stands behind our wall; looking through the windows, gazing through the lattice." Get a picture of this in your mind. In this verse, we see Jesus on the outside looking in. That's the way it is in many of our churches today. He's standing outside, behind the wall that we've built. The lattice was built to keep the vines out, but instead, we've used it to keep God out, so He doesn't get too close to us. We're "walled in." You've heard the saying, "Don't put God in a box." Well, He can't be put in a box. We're the ones that are in the box. Until we open up to Him and let Him into every area of our lives He remains on the outside looking in.

Do you remember what Jesus said to the church at Laodicea in Revelation 3:20? He said, "Behold, I stand at the door and knock. If anyone hears My voice and opens the door, I will come in to him and dine with him, and he with Me." He was on the outside. He wasn't on the inside. The church of Laodicea symbolizes the end-time church. Unfortunately, many churches have left Jesus on the outside. We must be determined to let Him in. He's standing at the door. He's knocking. He's looking in through the lattice. Will we let Him come in and have His way? He beckons us, just like the king beckoned to the Shulamite woman in verse 10.

RISE UP MY LOVE!

Song of Solomon 2:10 (NKJV)
My beloved spoke, and said to me: "Rise up, my love, my fair one, and come away.

He's beckoning her to stop hiding behind the walls. He's calling for her to put away all of her inhibitions and to rise up and come away with him. That's what the Lord is saying to His Church in these last days. There are new places to go. There is a shift taking place, and we must rise to the occasion as He calls us to that higher place with Him.

THE WINTER IS PAST

Song of Solomon 2:11-12 (NKJV)
11 For lo, the winter is past, the rain is over and gone.

12 The flowers appear on the earth; the time of singing has come, and the voice of the turtledove is heard in our land.

We all go through seasons in our lives. There are seasons of change and seasons of growth. The king says, "The winter is past." Can I speak that word prophetically into your life? Can you receive that as a word from the Lord? The winter is past! This is God's *rhema* word for His Church... for His Bride. He is singing over you and prophesying over you that your winter is over. All the harshness and all the coldness of the past has come to an end. The rain is over and gone. The flowers are now springing up and the time of singing has come. This is where the body of Christ is right now. Spring has come!

You're entering into a new season. The storms that came into your life to beat you and to torment you are gone now. Wintertime is over and springtime is here. Blossoms are blooming. Once-barren tree limbs are budding, and flowers are appearing. You've been fed with apples from God's Word, now you're about to start producing fruit on your limbs that others can come and partake of. The spring of your life has come.

Yes, the Bride of Christ is being called out of her old ways and she's being called into a new season... to a new dispensation. But, we must remember, when God took the Israelites out of Egypt He also had to take Egypt out of the Israelites. We've got to get Egypt out of our thinking. We have to put the slave mentality behind us so we can see ourselves as He sees us. He's brought us into the Promised Land. Winter is past. Our slavery is over. Hardship and struggle is no more. Spring has come and it's a season of singing, rejoicing and celebration.

Song of Solomon 2:13 (NKJV)
The fig tree puts forth her green figs, and the vines with the tender grapes give a good smell. Rise up, my love, my fair one, and come away!

Throughout the scriptures figs are representative of the nation of Israel. So, we see that as the Bride of Christ gets in her proper position in these last days, there will be an end-time harvest in the nation of Israel. Jesus is calling out to us, "Rise up, my love, my fair one, and come away!" Oh, the time is getting near for His return!

CHAPTER 6
YOUR FACE IS LOVELY

In this chapter, we're going to hone in on four specific verses... the last four verses of Song of Solomon, chapter 2.

Song of Solomon 2:14 (NKJV)
"O my dove, in the clefts of the rock, in the secret places of the cliff, let me see your face, let me hear your voice; for your voice is sweet, and your face is lovely."

Those are the words of King Solomon spoken to the Shulamite woman, but they are also the words of Jesus, our King, spoken to us, the Bride of Christ. In response to these words from the king, the Shulamite woman says:

Song of Solomon 2:15-17 (NKJV)
15 Catch us the foxes, the little foxes that spoil the vines, for our vines have tender grapes.
16 My beloved is mine, and I am his. He feeds his flock among the lilies.
17 Until the day breaks and the shadows flee away, turn, my beloved, and be like a gazelle or a young stag upon the mountains of Bether.

MY DOVE

Take note that in verse 14, the king calls the Shulamite woman "my dove." You might remember in chapter 1 verse 15, he said, "You have dove's eyes." There is such beautiful symbolism in comparing his beloved to a dove.

I mentioned this earlier, doves have no peripheral vision. They can only see what is directly in front of them. That is why it is so apropos that he said "You have dove's eyes." Her focus was to be directly upon him without any distraction. But, now, he's not only saying she has dove's eyes, he's telling her she *is* his dove.

Doves are symbolic of purity, innocence and loyalty. Oftentimes we don't see ourselves as pure or innocent, because we tend to look at our sins and imperfections. We tend to look at the "old man" we once were, instead of the new person that God created us to be. That's why the phrase "Oh my dove" is so important. This is the way God feels about us. This is the way He sees us. He says, "You are my dove. You are my pure, innocent dove." There's no place for our self-loathing and self-condemnation. There's no place for a poor self-image. The way He sees us is the way we should see ourselves.

Another interesting quality about doves is that they have a unique loyalty. They mate for life. If you recall, I mentioned in an earlier chapter how I had a pair of doves who used to come to the bird feeder at my house. One day, a hawk swooped down and got one of them. After that day, whenever I'd look out my window at the bird feeder I'd see the one dove by itself, all alone. That's because they mate for life. In light of that, Jesus says, "You are my dove. I am married to you for life." In Isaiah, He says, "I will betroth you to me forever." So, it's not just for this life, but it's for eternity. We are the *eternal* Bride of Christ.

I've said it before, but I need to reiterate it. If Satan can steal your identity, he can steal your destiny. The reason this teaching is so vital in this hour is that we, the Church, need to come into our end-time identity as the warrior Bride of Christ. If we don't come into that identity, Satan can steal our destiny. We must see ourselves as the Lord sees us. He says, "You are my dove. I am married to you for eternity. You are my eternal bride."

LET ME SEE YOUR FACE!

Song of Solomon 2:14 (NKJV)
"... in the clefts of the rock, in the secret places of the cliff, let me see your face, let me hear your voice; for your voice is sweet, and your face is lovely."

This is the place where a lot of Christians get stuck, until they get healed from their past. A lot of people, when they first come to Jesus, come with their head hanging down. This is because they're still living under the dark cloud of sin, shame, guilt and condemnation. Their eyes haven't switched focus yet to the way God sees them. So, God says to them, "You're in the secret place, in the cleft of the rock, so let me see your face." He's calling her to lift her face up.

My home state, New Jersey, has prophetically been called "The Face-to-Face State" so this is a very timely message to the Body of Christ in New Jersey. We are coming into a place where we are looking face-to-face with our God. We can't do that until we know who we are, until we are able to release all of the condemnation and guilt of the past. That guilt and condemnation causes us to hang our head. He wants us to lift our head so He can see our face.

Psalm 3:3 says, "You, O Lord, are a shield for me, my glory and the One who lifts up my head." God wants to lift your head. Religion wants you to bow your head. Religion beats you down and reminds you how sinful you are. Religion says you've got to pay a price to get God's approval. But I've got good news... the price has already been paid! Jesus paid the dowry for His Bride. Now we're free to look Him in the eyes. We're free to come before the Throne of Grace.

IN THE CLEFT OF THE ROCK

He says, "In the clefts of the rock, in the secret places of the cliff, let me see your face." Jesus has been called "The Rock." Do you remember the old song, "Rock of Ages, cleft for me?" Jesus is the eternal Rock, and He hides us in the cleft of the rock where we are protected and sheltered from harm and danger. The cleft of the rock is where the rock has been carved out. It's where it's been chiseled. God says, "Go in there and find My protection and shelter."

First Corinthians 10:4 eludes to the fact that Jesus is the rock being spoken of in Song of Solomon.

1 Corinthians 10:4 (NKJV)
And all drank the same spiritual drink. For they drank of that spiritual Rock that followed them, and that Rock was Christ.

Now, the cleft of the rock is symbolic of the wounds in Jesus' side. He says, "I want you hidden in my wounds. I received wounds so you could be free from yours. I want you to hide in that place that's been carved into my side. I am your Rock and you are My dove.

Colossians 3:3 (NKJV)
For you died, and your life is hidden with Christ in God.

Yes, He wants to *hide* you in His side, in that secret place. During wedding ceremonies, ministers often give reference to the fact that God used a rib from Adam's side to create Eve. He didn't take a bone from Adam's foot, to symbolize that man would rule over woman. Nor did He take a bone from his head, to symbolize that woman would rule over man. No, the bone was taken from his side, symbolizing that man and woman are to be side-by-side, arm-in-arm, working together as one flesh.

In Exodus 33:14, God said to Moses, "My Presence will go with you." In response to those words, Moses said to God, "Please, show me Your glory." Moses was saying, "If You're going to show me Your Presence, then show me Your Glory." That's because God's Presence and His Glory are inseparable. God answered Moses' request in a very interesting way.

Exodus 33:22 (NKJV)
So it shall be, while My glory passes by, that I will put you in the cleft of the rock, and will cover you with My hand while I pass by.

You will not see His glory until you get in the cleft of the Rock. There are a lot of ministries that say they want to see Jesus, but they're not hiding in the wounds of the Lamb. They're not in the cleft. They're not in that secret place. There's a reason He calls it a "secret place." Not everyone finds it. So, tuck yourself into Jesus' side and you will see God's Glory.

THE KEVOD OF GOD

The word "glory" is the Hebrew word *kevod*. You can be in meetings where people are jumping around and dancing and you might say, "The Glory of God is here." No. That's more of a party atmosphere. Let me straighten out the confusion about this. When God's Glory comes, when the *kevod* of God comes, you won't be able to dance. It's heavy. It's weighty. You can't stand in it. It's thick and hot, like molasses. It's liquid love. It weighs you down. Think about all the times in the Bible where men encountered God in all His Glory and fell as dead men. It's an overwhelming, over-powering event.

Many years ago I was opening up one of our women's Bible study meetings, and I picked up the mic to start the meeting with an opening prayer. From out of nowhere, the *kevod* of God came upon me. Slowly but surely I "melted" down to the floor and it felt like I was super-glued to the carpet. I couldn't even lift a pinky. Still having some presence of mind, I thought within myself, "I sure hope this is hitting everybody else and they're not just sitting out there watching me, wondering what's going on." I was able to lift one eye and I looked out to see the whole room full of ladies on their faces, plastered to the floor. That's the Glory! We can't withstand His Glory because of the imperfections in us. Our flesh can't handle it. But, He gives us a glimpse of His Glory by offering us that secret hiding place in Christ's side. It's not until we're securely tucked away in the cleft of the Rock that He reveals His Glory. He says, "When you get in the cleft, then the Glory will come."

There are lots of ministers and pastors who don't know what to do when that sort of thing happens. They get uncomfortable. Listen, when you say, "Show me Your Glory," you've got to know what you're saying. It's such a weighty, heavy thing that happens. We've got to get tucked into Jesus' side; hidden away in that secret place in the wounds of the Lamb before we can behold His Glory. We can't get in His Glory with our flesh imperfections. It's only through the blood of Jesus. That blood covers us so we can get in His Presence.

Psalm 91:1-2 (NKJV)
1 He who dwells in the secret place of the Most High shall abide under the shadow of the Almighty.
2 I will say of the Lord, "He is my refuge and my fortress; my God, in Him I will trust."

Take note that Psalm 91:1 talks about that secret place. It says, "He who *dwells* ...." That word dwells means "lives in, inhabits." You've got to stay there and abide there; tucked away in that secret place. When you dwell there, God says, "You shall abide under the shadow of the Almighty." Under His shadow, we find a place of protection. Listen, you can go through hell on earth, but if you're dwelling in that secret place in the cleft of the Rock, you're shielded, because you're in His presence.

LET ME

Song of Solomon 2:14 (NKJV)
"... let me see your face, let me hear your voice; for your voice is sweet, and your face is lovely."

Did you notice that God says the words "let me?" It sounds like somebody's got to give Him permission, doesn't it? You have to relinquish your will to Him. He's asking for your permission. God Almighty is asking to see your face. The One who created you in your mother's womb; the One who fashioned you and formed you is saying, "Let Me see the work I've created. Let me behold the beautiful creation I've made. Let me see your face. Let me hear your voice, for your voice is sweet and your face is lovely." He's saying, "Come out from behind the guilt, the shame, the fear and the condemnation, My Bride, and show Me your face."

When your kids come to you and you just want to love on them, but their head is hanging down, and they're looking dejected, you say, "Come here. Look at me." That's what God wants to do to you. He wants to lift your head so He can look you in the eyes. Fear hides its face and fear doesn't speak. Neither does guilt or shame. The devil wants your head hanging down and your mouth shut, but God says, "Let me *see* your face... let Me *hear* your voice."

FULLY ASSURED

Hebrews 10:19 (NIV)
Therefore, brothers and sisters, since we have confidence to enter

the Most Holy Place by the blood of Jesus...

That's how we can come before God. That's how we can worship Him without shame or guilt. It's through the blood of Jesus. That's how we enter into that Holy Place with Him. It's not on my own merit. It's not because of anything I've done. It's all because of Jesus. I know that God can't wait to see me. He wants to see my face and hear my voice. It's not because I have some kind of great prayer life. I don't. I just say, "I'm here!" That's my prayer life! "I'm here and I want to be with You, Lord, and I know You want to be with me, too." Everything else that happens in my prayer time is just a result of that desire to be in His Presence.

Hebrews 10:20-23 (NIV)
20 ... by a new and living way opened for us through the curtain, that is, his body
21 and since we have a great priest over the house of God,
22 let us draw near to God with a sincere heart and with the full assurance that faith brings, having our hearts sprinkled to cleanse us from a guilty conscience and having our bodies washed with pure water.
23 Let us hold unswervingly to the hope we profess, for he who promised is faithful.

Fully assured. I'm fully assured that He wants to be with me. Fully assured that He loves me. Fully assured that He wants to see my face and hear my voice. How do you get that full assurance? The rest of the verse gives the answer... "having our hearts sprinkled to cleanse us from a guilty conscience." The thing that's keeping you out of God's Presence is a guilty conscience. But God tells us that Jesus shed His blood to wash that away.

Jesus washed the disciples' feet because they had been out there walking around in the world. He wants to cleanse us, too. We're coming into contact with the world every day. The uncleanness in this world has a tendency to rub off on us. So, we come to Jesus to get washed; to get rid of that guilty conscience, so we can hold on unswervingly to the hope we profess. He who promised is faithful!

God even takes things a step further in 1 John 3:20.

1 John 3:20 (NIV)
If our hearts condemn us, we know that God is greater than our hearts, and he knows everything.

Is your heart condemning you. God is greater than your heart. He knows what you've been through. He knows how you got where you are today. He knows what happened to you this past week and how it affected you. He's greater than that! Amen!

LET ME HEAR YOUR VOICE

Let's look a little closer at Song of Solomon 2:14:

Song of Solomon 2:14 (NKJV)
"... let me see your face, let me hear your voice; for your voice is sweet, and your face is lovely."

He not only says, "Let me see your face," He also says, "Let me hear your voice." The devil wants to silence you. He wants you to keep your mouth shut. He says, "You're no good. You don't deserve to talk to God. I heard you say that cuss word. I know the way you really are." Listen, the same devil that talks to me, talks to you. He doesn't have any new tricks. I've heard all of his accusations. That's why I make frequent use of the phrase "Talk to the hand," when he's trying to talk to me. It would do you good to do the same. When you hear Satan's voice of accusation coming against you, stick your hand out and say, "Talk to the hand! I'm not listening to you!"

God wants to hear your voice. He wants to hear your adoring

praise and worship. Not because He's on some kind of ego trip. No! He knows when you praise Him you get refocused. You get your eyes off of everything else and you focus on how big and powerful and awesome He is. God says, "Your prayers are like incense to Me." That's why He wants to hear your voice. It blesses Him because He loves hearing you.

I've heard some people say, "You can pray with your mouth shut." Well, "Yes" and "No." There are some instances when you can't pray out loud. For example, in China, there are places where Christians have to pray under their breath, because if they prayed out loud they could be imprisoned or even murdered. But if you live in a free country, God says, "Let me hear your voice. Your words in prayer become powerful weapons. Your words have creative power. When you speak My words there is spirit and life in them. I want to hear your voice."

God is your glory and the lifter of your head. The enemy wants to beat you down. People who have been abused verbally, physically and emotionally are all bottled up inside. That's the way the devil wants them to stay. But, God wants them to open up to Him. God wants them to release words to Him that will free them up from their past hurts and failures. He's calling out to us, "Open up to me. Open up to me. Don't keep everything bottled up inside you. I want to hear your voice!"

THE LITTLE FOXES

How does the Shulamite woman respond to these words from the king?

Song of Solomon 2:15 (NKJV)
Catch us the foxes, the little foxes that spoil the vines, for our vines have tender grapes.

This is a desperate cry for deliverance. "Deliver me. Help Me."

Listen, sometimes you have to *fight* to get your fight back. I've been there. I've felt so beat down that I didn't have the strength to fight, but I knew I had to fight. So, I had to *fight* just to get my fight back. That's what's going on with the Shulamite woman here. She's crying out for help and deliverance so she can get back to the place where she has some fight in her. What's hindering her? What problem is she facing? It's not monumental problems. It's the "little foxes." It's the small, hidden areas of life that cause fear and compromise. They're keeping her from giving her total focus to her relationship with the king.

Foxes are cunning, sneaky, crafty animals. They're quick and very difficult to catch. They come out at night to steal and to plunder the crops. They don't come out in the daytime where you can see them. That's what makes them so sneaky and hard to catch. That's why we have expressions like "Sly as a fox," and "You can't outfox a fox." She's crying out, "Catch them for me. I can't do it alone." These little foxes are the little areas of your life that keep you from one hundred percent commitment and complete abandonment to the Lord. They're the areas of compromise that sneak in and try to ruin all that you and the Lord have been working for. We tend to focus on the really big things in our lives... the blatant, out-right sins. While we're working on those major issues, however, these little areas of compromise are eating our fruit and destroying our vineyard.

Not only should we give God the big issues in our lives, but we must surrender the small ones as well. We shouldn't leave any stone unturned. We must give the Holy Spirit access to every area of our lives, and say, "Take those little foxes away, Lord."

Foxes eat unripened grapes. If you don't get the foxes out of the vineyard, they will dig out a den beneath the grapevines and have their babies there. While the mother fox is out eating the grapes, the babies are chewing on the roots and the bottom of the vine. They're sitting there sucking the juice out of the vine. That's why the Shulamite woman cries out for help, "Catch us the foxes, the little foxes that spoil the vine."

It's those little areas of compromise that you allow in your life that will leave you barren, with a fruitless vine. You're working hard to try to run off the adult foxes, not realizing that the baby foxes are underground eating your vine. All of this is happening while the vineyards are in blossom. It's a critical time as you're developing fruit for God's kingdom. God wants to help you get rid of all those little distractions and irritations so you can be fruitful. Cry out to Him and He will deliver you from all those pesky little areas in your life.

Before we move on to the next verse, there's one more thing I want you to see in this one. Notice that she says, "for *our* vineyards have tender grapes." She calls them "ours." She's starting to realize that God has a stake in her life. It's not just *her* vineyard to care for anymore... it's *their* vineyard. She's saying, "Jesus, you have invested so much in this vineyard, this isn't just *mine* anymore... it's *ours*!"

HE IS MINE... I AM HIS

Song of Solomon 2:16 (NKJV)
My beloved is mine, and I am his. He feeds his flock among the lilies.

Do you remember in Song of Solomon 1, when the Shulamite woman asked the king, "Tell me where do you feed your flock?" He responded to her question by saying, "Follow the footsteps of the sheep." Later on, he brought her to the banqueting house, to his table. In doing this, he physically showed her the place where he fed his flock. She sat at his table and experienced his provision first hand. So now, in verse 16, we get an even better description of the place where he feeds his flocks... "among the lilies."

In the last chapter I talked extensively about the symbolic meaning behind lilies. I mentioned that lilies have over 50 bulbs under the ground, symbolically reminding us that there is so much more to the people we meet than what meets the eye. This is why we shouldn't judge others, because we can't see the hidden things that God is doing in their lives. God says, "I feed my flock among the lilies. When I feed my sheep you can't see all that's growing inside of them. You can't see all that they're becoming as I'm nurturing them with My Word."

Now, I want you to take note of how verse 16 is phrased, "My beloved is mine, and I am his." The reason I call attention to this is because there is a progression taking place throughout Song of Solomon. When we first meet the Shulamite woman she is very self-centered. She is focused on her deficiencies and inadequacies. She becomes aware of the king's love for her and their relationship grows. In chapter 1 verse 14, she says, "My beloved is to me…." She's only aware of her own needs being met in this relationship to start with. She's a self-centered person, a self-centered bride at first. But, she is on her way to becoming a mature bride. This is where the Body of Christ is right now. Unfortunately, we're more "me-focused" than "God-focused." We're more aware of what this relationship with the Lord has done *for* us and *to* us. When we first got saved, we said, "He's *my* best friend, He's *my* Lord. He's *my* Savior." We're saying, "This is what He is to *me*." The emphasis is placed on "me" and "my."

When she says, "My beloved is to me…" she hasn't acknowledged His rights to her. She only recognizes the benefits she's received from him. This is the way we are when we first get born again. It's called being a "baby Christian." Her main focus is on His love for her, and on all the goodies she received when she got saved. But, when we get to verse 16 of chapter 2, she says, "My beloved is mine, and I am his." Ah! We're beginning to see a little bit of growth here. She's beginning to add a new dimension to their relationship. She's recognizing his ownership of her life. She's saying, "He belongs to me, but I also *belong to Him*."

Recognizing this progression will bring new revelation to our worship times. Let me explain. If you go to a church and listen to their worship songs, you can get an idea if that church is a baby church or a mature church. Listen to the words being sung in worship. If there is a major focus on "me" and "I" then you're most likely in a baby church. That kind of worship is "me-focused." "I am redeemed," "I am...," "I am...." But, when you're in a mature church, the worship is more God-focused. "He is" and "Lord, You are" are the words being lifted up to God in worship. There's nothing wrong with being a baby in the Lord, but He wants us to grow in our relationship with Him so we can become a mature Bride. If we only worship Him because of all the goodies, and all that He's done for us, and all that we can do because of Him, we're missing the higher level of relationship that He's calling us to. God wants a mature bride.

So we see in verse 16 that she begins to recognize his ownership of her as she says, "I am his." Unfortunately, it is a secondary thought. Her first thought is still "My beloved is mine." But, at least we're starting to see some maturity in her. I want to ask you... in which stage of this progression do you find yourself? Are you an immature bride or a mature bride? Be honest with yourself when you answer that question. Are you more focused on your benefits and ownership in the relationship, or are you surrendering yourself to His ownership?

Later on, in chapter 6 verse 3, she says, "I am my beloved's, and he is mine." The ownership and priorities get switched. She reaches a new maturity level in chapter 6 as she recognizes his ownership first, yet she still holds on to her own ownership in the relationship. She's still holding on to her inheritance in him, and it's important to her, but at least it becomes secondary.

Moving forward in Song of Solomon, there is still another step toward maturity that she takes in chapter 7 verse 10 when she says, "I am my beloved's, and his desire is for me." There is no "He is mine" mentioned. She's saying, "I am his and his desire is for me, but I don't own him anymore. I don't have rights to him. It's not all about me anymore. I exist for him. My focus is on him. He is the source of my love. I am rooted in the revelation of his passion for me."

A PREPARED BRIDE

You will never become a passionate worshipper, nor will you ever become a passionate bride, until you have the revelation of His passionate love for you. I worship passionately because I have the revelation that He is madly in love with me. He wants to see my face. He wants to hear my voice. He waits at the altar for me.

At a wedding ceremony, you don't see the bride at the altar. No! The groom is at the altar waiting for the bride to come into the room. He's waiting to get a glimpse of her as she first enters the room.

The most beautiful wedding I ever witnessed was that of my son, Mark, and his wife, Melissa. I remember Mark was so afraid that he was going to see Melissa before the ceremony started because we had a couple of mishaps before the wedding began. He didn't want to see her until she was completely ready. He wanted to see her in all her glory and beauty. He said to me, "Don't tell me anything, Mom. Don't tell me how she looks. I want it to be a surprise." I said only one thing to him… "Sheer perfection!" She was the most beautiful bride I had ever seen.

Jesus waits at the altar. He's waiting for a Bride who is prepared for her wedding day, decked out in all her glory… sheer perfection. The world looks on and says, "Who is this coming up out of the wilderness; I've never seen a church look like that before. That doesn't look like tradition or religion. She's leaning on her beloved. She's walking in the confidence of who she is, as the end-time Bride of Christ. She's a warrior Bride. Just look at her!"

This is where He is taking us. He's taking us out of our old, religious ways. Winter has passed. Springtime has come. The time of singing and celebration has come. Whatever He desires, whatever He wants, I am my beloved's and his passionate desire is for me.

When Jesus hung on that cross and died, He cried out, "It is finished!" Study it. It means, "I've purchased a bride!" That's the literal Greek translation... "It's a bride." Back before pregnant mothers could discover the sex of their baby before birth, when the baby finally arrived, an announcement was made... "It's a boy!" or "It's a girl!" Well, right before Jesus breathed His last breath on the cross, He cried out, "It's a bride!" You can't earn that. Religion is done. Tradition is done. Condemnation and guilt are gone. The bride has been purchased. The work is accomplished through Christ. It is finished!

I'm in love with Him and He's in love with me, and that settles it, completely. I am His Bride. I am Mrs. Jesus Christ. I say those words often... "I am Mrs. Jesus Christ!" When I say it, I can hear every religious demon exclaim, "Whaaaat?! Blasphemy! How can you say that?" I can say it because I'm the Bride of Christ. He's given me His name.

Listen, you've got to rise up to this identity in this hour. You are not a beat up, backslidden, little fox-eaten vine. You're a devil-stomping, Holy Ghost filled, destined and empowered, liberated, set free, wife of the Most High God!

A PASSIONATE BRIDE

No man in his right mind wants a wife that's completely bound up and frigid. There isn't a sane man on the face of this earth that doesn't want a red-hot, passionate wife. Where do you think that desire came from? It came from the King! Those are God's desires. This will cure every marriage. I just gave you some free marriage counseling right there. Just think about what would happen in our relationships if we would move from being self-centered to God-centered. Just look at your spouse and say, "Let me see your face. Let me hear your voice. I love your kisses. Your kisses are better than wine. Your face is sweet. Your voice is lovely." Any woman in her right mind would agree that this kind of talk and interaction from her spouse would create passion within her. You see, it goes both ways. Husbands want a passionate wife, and wives want a passionate husband. God is passionate for us, and we should be passionate for Him, too!

He loves us, and there's no higher calling in life than loving Him. If this world could see that kind of passionate interaction between Christians and the Lord it would set them free. When we're passionate for Him we're representing Him correctly. In the past we've misrepresented Him with all of our tradition and religion. The world needs to see this love relationship.

I'll ask you this question: "Do you see yourself as a sinner who sometimes loves God, or do you see yourself as a lover of God who sometimes sins?" Picture yourself standing before Jesus. How do you see yourself? Do you see yourself as someone He is passionately, even madly, in love with? Or, do you see yourself beat up and hanging your head? If He spoke to you, what do you think He would say to you? Can you hear Him speak words of tender love and affection, or do you think they would be words of rebuke and condemnation? The last time you went and prayed, what was that like? Were you begging, pleading with God, just hoping He'd listen to your prayer? Were you so filled with guilt and shame that it kept you from even entering into His presence? Or, were you so aware of His love for you that you couldn't wait to enter into His presence? Does your view of yourself match up to His view of you? It's important that you see the way He feels about you. It affects your perspective. This perspective is the lens through which you see life. When you see yourself from God's perspective it will change your life. It will change your marriage. It will change the way you see yourself.

A NEW DAY IS HERE!

Let's look at the final verse of Song of Solomon chapter 2. This is the Shulamite woman speaking to the king.

Song of Solomon 2:17 (NKJV)
Until the day breaks and the shadows flee away, Turn, my beloved, and be like a gazelle or a young stag upon the mountains of Bether.

"Until the day breaks…." I can look at this two different ways. The first way I look at it is the dawning of the new day when Christ returns to Earth. But, let's break it down another way. Let's bring it into where we live right now. There's a dawning of a new day coming in our lives, and in our spiritual walk. The winter is past and it's the dawn of something new right now. The light is breaking forth and the darkness is leaving… the shadows are fleeing away. Aren't you ready for a new day in your life?

Bether literally means "separation." So she's crying out, "Until that Day breaks, I want you to come into those places in my life that have separated me from you." We cry out to the Lord with that same prayer, "Lord, come into the places in my life that have separated me from You." Bether was a mountain in Palestine. The root meaning of the name Bether is derived from the parts of the animal that were cut in half for sacrifice. So, when we speak of Bether, we're saying, "Lord, everything that separates me from You, You've paid the sacrifice for. There once was a mountain of separation between the two of us, but through Your sacrifice, You have leaped across the separation, like a gazelle, to bridge the gap between us." You see, He's not only your eternal Bridegroom, He is also your eternal sacrifice. That's huge! That means you never have to pay the price again. It's a done deal! It's a new day. It's a new time. Winter is past.

Listen, when God does a work of restoration, He doesn't just start all over. He brings things to full restoration and makes them better than they were originally intended to be. This is where we are today. A new day is breaking. We're in the day of the restoration of the church. This is the time of the restoration of the Bride of Christ. Let Him see your face... you are lovely to Him!

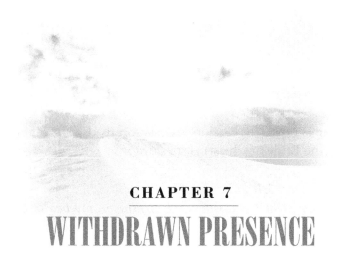

CHAPTER 7
WITHDRAWN PRESENCE

In this chapter, we're going to focus specifically on 5 verses – Song of Solomon 3:1-5. I want us to look at these five verses both in the New International Version and The Passion Translation. I will preface the verses with a note about who is doing the speaking in each section. To begin with, the Shulamite woman is speaking in the following verses.

Song of Solomon 3:1-4 (NIV)
1 All night long on my bed I looked for the one my heart loves; I looked for him but did not find him.
2 I will get up now and go about the city, through its streets and squares; I will search for the one my heart loves. So I looked for him but did not find him.
3 The watchmen found me as they made their rounds in the city. "Have you seen the one my heart loves?"
4 Scarcely had I passed them when I found the one my heart loves. I held him and would not let him go till I had brought him to my mother's house, to the room of the one who conceived me.

The king responds with a word of admonishment to the daughters of Jerusalem. Remember, the daughters of Jerusalem are symbolic of the "onlookers" in our life who are watching our relationship with the Lord.

Song of Solomon 3:5 (NIV)
Daughters of Jerusalem, I charge you by the gazelles and by the does of the field: do not arouse or awaken love until it so desires.

Now, here is how The Passion Translation reads. The Shulamite woman (the Bride of Christ) is speaking:

Song of Solomon 3:1-4 (TPT)
1 Night after night I'm tossing and turning on my bed of travail. Why did I let him go from me? How my heart now aches for him, but he is nowhere to be found!
2 So I must rise in search of him, looking throughout the city, seeking until I find him. Even if I have to roam through every street, nothing will keep me from my search. Where is he—my soul's true love? He is nowhere to be found.
3 Then I encountered the overseers as they encircled the city. So I asked them, "Have you found him—my heart's true love?"
4 Just as I moved past them, I encountered him. I found the one I adore! I caught him and fastened myself to him, refusing to be feeble in my heart again. Now I'll bring him back to the temple within where I was given new birth—into my innermost parts, the place of my conceiving.

The king replies:

Song of Solomon 3:5 (TPT)
Promise me, O Jerusalem maidens, by the gentle gazelles and delicate deer, that you'll not disturb my love until she is ready to arise.

Song of Solomon melts my heart each time I read it as I see God's love for His Bride prophetically tucked away in its passages. So, let's go over this verse by verse and I will explain what is happening, both "in the natural" and also prophetically.

Song of Solomon 3:1 (NIV)
All night long on my bed I looked for the one my heart loves; I looked for him but did not find him.

Have you ever been in this place before? You're up all night long, not able to sleep because there's a strong yearning in your heart for God, but His Presence seems so far away? When you're sensitive to His Presence and He withdraws His Presence, it *should* keep you awake. His Presence should be your lifeline. His Presence brings you peace and joy. There's nothing like His Presence. Once you've experienced it you can no longer be content without it. This Shulamite woman had been in the presence of the king, but now he is nowhere to be found. In the darkness of the night hours, she realizes how much she misses his presence.

NIGHT SEASONS

We all deal with night seasons in our lives. Night seasons are times of darkness and uncertainty that we experience. It's difficult to see what's going on around us during these night seasons. The Church, historically, has gone through dark periods in its history. You've heard of "The Dark Ages," right? During the Dark Ages the church didn't know where God was. It was a time of darkness and uncertainty. I'm so thankful that our night seasons don't last as long as they did during the Dark Ages!

A KISS OF DISCIPLINE AND CORRECTION

The Shulamite woman said, "I looked for him but could not find him." That's because the king had intentionally withdrawn his presence from her in hopes to draw her to himself. Likewise, the Lord will withdraw His Presence from our lives so He can woo us unto Himself. I know what you're thinking. The Lord said He'd never leave us nor forsake us, so why would He remove His Presence from us? What you need to understand is this is actually a divine kiss of discipline and correction. In the case of the Shulamite woman, the king had been calling her up to the mountains with Him. Remember the mountain of Bether mentioned at the end of Chapter 2? He had been calling her up higher, but she declined the offer. She has been disobedient to his wooing and now she feels his absence, and is desperate to be in his presence once more.

Yes, as the church, we too have received this kiss of discipline and correction, at one time or another. The Bride is now entering a period of time of discipline for her disobedience. Maybe this doesn't pertain to you right now, but you can probably think of other people or churches who are in this position at the moment. The Lord has called them to come up to the mountain, but they have denied Him.

There are many reasons why people reject God's call for greater intimacy with Him. Some are too comfortable and complacent where they are currently. Maybe they're in a preoccupied, lazy place in their lives. Maybe even a worldly place that they just don't want to surrender to the Lord completely.

The Lord is calling the Church to come up higher. He's saying, "Rise up my love, my fair one, and come away with me." As shown here in the Song of Solomon, He calls us to Himself by withdrawing His presence from us. He steps back. He pulls away. But, He's not pulling away to reject us. No! He's pulling away because of His great love for us. He withdraws His presence, not for rejection... but for correction.

WHY WOULD GOD WITHDRAW HIS PRESENCE?

Sometimes God will withdraw His presence to show you what you've been missing. The withdrawal of His presence creates a deeper hunger and desire for Him. It creates a holy dissatisfaction inside of you and a desperation that makes you want to say, "I can't stay here any longer. I've got to be where He is. I repent for staying in my comfort zone. I repent for my complacency. I want His presence more than my own comfort." That's where we find the Shulamite woman in this verse. She realizes how much she misses her lover. She was in his presence but now he's nowhere to be found. She looked for him in her bed, in the place of intimacy, but could not find him. She misses his presence and is now ready to passionately pursue him.

God loves us so much that He will not leave us the way He found us. Don't get me wrong. He'll take us, just the way we are. But, He loves you too much to leave us that way. He has more that He wants us to experience. He wants to take us to a higher place in Him.

COME UP HERE

How is He going to get us to that place? One of the ways He does it is by creating a holy desperation and dissatisfaction within us. How does He do that? By withdrawing His presence from us. In Revelation chapter 4 verse 1, and chapter 11 verse 12, the Lord is speaking to the end-time church saying, "Come up here." Basically, He was saying, "There are some things I want to show you, but I can't show you down there... you've got to come up here, where I am, to see it." He said, "Come up here" to the apostle John in Revelation 4:1. Upon hearing those words, this is what happened to John, in his own words: "Immediately I was in the Spirit; and behold a throne set in heaven, and One sat on the throne" (Revelation 4:2). When God calls you to come up higher you can see Him in His greater glory, as the One who sits upon the throne. That's where I want to be! In His presence, before His throne! God wants to show us (the Bride of Christ) what things look like from His perspective. He wants to show us things to come.

The end-time Bride of Christ is not prepared for what is coming. She's not ready yet. So, He is wooing her and saying, "Come up higher. Come to where I am." God must allow times in our lives where we have a discontentment in our heart. We must become so dissatisfied with ordinary Christianity (if there is such a thing). We can become so comfortable in our born-again, resurrection-life experience that it becomes commonplace to us. We take it for granted. It becomes ordinary, instead of extraordinary. It becomes rote. We religiously say, "I go to church on Sunday morning. This is my obligation. This is what I do." Instead, we should be saying, "I don't *go* to church, I *am* the church. I'm in a living, thriving, passionate relationship with my King!" Our holy discontentment will cause us to rise up and begin searching. We won't stay in the place where we are. He's always calling us higher.

WHAT'S "HOLDING YOU UP?"

Now, something else I should mention about the night time is that it is a time where we are free from the distractions of the day. God will allow you to go into a night season where He will remove all the props. All the things you've become dependent on, all the things you've been leaning on, and all the things that have been holding you up need to be taken away. You need to be in a place where you realize all that's holding you up is His arms. Remember in Song of Solomon 2:6, where the king held the Shulamite woman in his embrace? That's what needs to happen in our lives. All the superficial props that we think hold us up need to be removed. You thought it was your pastor that was holding you up. You thought it was your best friend that was holding you up. But, in the night season, when you're by yourself, and all alone, you come to realize that it is Him. He's the One who's been holding you up. All of the distractions and cares of daily life are removed in those dark, night-time hours, so you can see things the way they
really are.

At the end of Chapter 2, the Shulamite woman was talking about *our* vineyards. She finally came to the place where she realized God had ownership over her life. It was no longer "me and mine," – it was "ours." But when you look at Song of Solomon 3:1, you see she's gone back to the singular possessive talk. She says, "All night long on *my* bed…." She's calling it *my* bed, not *our* bed. Who left the bed? He withdrew himself and she was feeling all alone and isolated, so now she's in a place of desperation.

You know, when I see someone at that point I don't get in God's way. I won't awaken or arouse love before it's ready, and you shouldn't either. Are you hearing that? You see, God is wooing them. God is calling them higher. Don't interfere with that. Let them grow desperate. Let them get dissatisfied. Let them get hungry. Don't try to be the Holy Spirit or take over His job. It's the job of the Holy Spirit to draw people to God, so don't try to arouse or awaken love before it's ready.

WHEN LOVE PULLS AWAY

So here the Shulamite woman is. She can't sleep because the withdrawing of the manifest presence of God is now creating a desire in her that is so powerful that it's causing her to seek Him even when it's inconvenient. She has to get out of her comfortable bed. She's been sleeping alone there for too long. She's been "laying down" in her Christianity for a while. She says, "I've got to get up. I've got to get myself up, even if it's inconvenient." She can't sleep. You see, love will pull away for a moment to pull the other person in.

Let me put this in physical, fleshly terms, just for a minute. If a person is single and extremely clingy to the person they're in a relationship with, it can be a real turn off. But, if they act cool, act just a little disinterested, and let the other person think they might be losing them, that adds some intrigue to the relationship. The other person will begin to pursue them with more intensity. The world calls it "playing hard to get." Well, God's not playing hard to get, but He definitely wants to increase the intrigue in His relationship with us.

Unfortunately, some don't even realize that the presence of God is missing from their lives and from their church services. They have a weekly ritual of church attendance where a religious obligation is fulfilled without ever pursuing God and His presence. They don't see that their relationship with the Lord is a vital union. They don't understand that going to a corporate church service is a chance to come together with others who have like passion and faith and desire to be with their King. Some have never tasted of the goodness of God so they are content with their empty religion at the expense of a true relationship. The scripture says, "Taste and see," but they've never tasted, so they don't know what they're missing.

Oh, but once you've tasted of God's presence, it's just like being a chocoholic… you've got to have more. You're not content with just a little bit. You want more, and more, and more. When you've tasted something good it should leave you wanting more. But if you've never tasted, then you don't know what you're missing. Some Christians love God with their minds, but not with their hearts. It's not an intimate experience. It's a mental one. Those who have tasted of Him are not content with religious ritual. Just like the Shulamite woman, they know what they're missing. They're willing to lose sleep in pursuit of Him. They're willing to be inconvenienced. They'll not give up until they find Him. "WHERE ARE YOU, GOD?"

I've been there. Perhaps you've been there, too. I've been to that place the Shulamite woman is, asking, "Where are you God? Where are You? I can't feel You. What's going on? Where did You go?" So, she starts seeking him the only way she knows how. "Maybe if I pray more. Maybe if I read my Bible more. Maybe if I start fasting, God will come back to me." But, after trying everything, she couldn't find Him. He's not looking for her to pray more, or to read the Bible more. He's not looking for her to fast. He wants her to come to where He is. He wants to have a relationship with her. A relationship that's not dependent on any of the religious props.

Listen, there are people who read the Bible and study it for hours, yet they have no relationship with Him. They don't know Him. They haven't found Him. And, here she is saying, "I've done everything I know to do but I still haven't found Him." Jesus disciplines her by withdrawing His presence.

When God calls you to do something, and you don't do it, it's called "disobedience." Spiritual disciplines such as Bible reading, praying and fasting can not take the place of obedience. Remember, God said, "Obedience is better than sacrifice." If God tells you to draw close to Him and you refuse to go to where He is, then you're in disobedience.

So, here we see God creating a greater desire in her heart, a greater desperation that will cause her to rise up into something new. That holy discontentment will raise her up into her destiny, to that place He has for her. She got saved, and she got baptized in the Holy Spirit. She went to the King's table, and she even went into His chambers, but then He withdrew Himself. Now she can't find Him so she says:

Song of Solomon 3:2 (NKJV)
"I will rise now," I said, "And go about the city; In the streets and in the squares I will seek the one I love." I sought him, but I did not find him.

NOW!

That little three-letter word "now" will change your life. I know I've got to get up. I know I've got to do something. But when am I going to do it? *Now!* Faith is always *now*. Hebrews 11:1 says, "*Now* faith is... *now* faith is...." Faith is never *tomorrow*. She said, "I will rise now. I have to obey what he said to me in Chapter 2 verse 13. 'Arise my love, my fair one, and come away with me.'"

Some people have had to leave their comfort zone in a dead

church in order to pursue the Lord. They had to leave the complacency, the ritual, and the comfort of a church that didn't require anything of their Christianity except to show up once a week and pay their tithes. They were called out of the traditions of their past in pursuit of a living relationship with Jesus.

She said, "I will rise *now*." She realized she was in a bad place and something needed to change quickly. Her eyes were opened and she knew she didn't have time to mess around. "I will rise *now*." Every one of us must come to this place. Everyone has to make that decision at one time or another in our life. Are we going to stay in the comfort zone of our dead religion, or are we going to rise up and obey the call of the Spirit to be that end-time Bride, that warring Bride that is destined to rule and reign with the King?

Read the book of Revelation. Jesus said to the churches, "I know your works. I know your deeds. Return to your first love. I'm standing at the door and knocking. Let me in." He's saying those same words to the Church today.

A KAIROS MOMENT

The word "now" is the Greek word *kairos*. It means "opportune time, a critical moment." We are at a critical moment in the Church. This is your *kairos* moment with God. You can't stay still in the kingdom of God. You're either moving forward or going backward. If you're not where He is then you're drying up–you're not moving forward. He's calling you to arise from your place of complacency to go where He is. *Now* is the time to do it!

If you choose to stay where you are, you'll be just like the frog that gets boiled in a pot of water. You can put a live frog in a pot of cold water and put it on the stove, and gradually turn the heat up until it boils. The frog won't jump out because the gradual change in temperature goes undetected. It will be boiled alive.

I've seen this happen in the Body of Christ. Slowly but surely churches are becoming desensitized to the things of the Spirit. They're becoming numb to God's presence, slowly being cooked in the pot. They're backsliding and they don't even know it. God's Word says, "Look how far you've fallen" (Revelation 2:5). It's time for the Church to arise!

Now, it's true that in Hebrews 13:5 God promised, "I will never leave you nor forsake you," but there are times we're not going to feel His presence. Why is that? It's because He wants to cause us to rise up and seek Him and pursue Him so He can bring us into the deeper and higher places He's calling us to. The Shulamite woman said, "I'm going to get off this bed of comfort, and I'm going to rise up and search for the one I love, so I can be where He is." How long you stay in that bed of comfort and complacency is completely up to you. You can stay there all night, or for weeks and months, or even for years.

YOUR LIFE DEPENDS ON IT

The word "rise" in Hebrew is actually a command. It means "to rise up from a reclining position as though your life depended on it." So when the Shulamite woman says, "I will rise up," she was saying, "My life depends on this." It's the same word used by the king when he says, "Rise up my love." God knows full well that when we rise up to meet Him our lives depend on it.

Her desperate response is "I will rise now and go about the city in the streets and squares to seek the one I love." So she went out looking for her lover, and she says, "I sought him, but I did not find him." She looked for him in her bed (in the place of intimacy) and could not find him. Then she looked for him in the public square, out among the people, and still could not find him.
The city, in verse 3, is a prophetic reference to the corporate church... to the city of God, if you will. She's leaving her bed of isolation, and she says, "I'll go where all the people are. Maybe

I will find my lover there." How many believers think they can serve God alone? It is a deception from the enemy. She begins to realize things aren't working for her on her own, so now she's going to where the people are. She's going into the city, to the local church, the congregation, and into the streets and squares. She's taking her search to the public arena. To the place where she works and interacts with other people. She's asking people, "Have you found the Lord? Do you know where I can find a good church? I can't find a good church, so I don't know where to go to find God's presence."

This is a picture of a desperate woman wandering through the streets at night. Have you ever felt that way? Have you ever felt like you're the only one who wants to go deeper with the Lord, but you can't find anyone who knows how, or is willing to go with you? Elijah felt that way. He was isolated in a cave saying, "Lord, I'm the only one left, and now they're trying to kill me." And God says, "Elijah, there are seven thousand more just like you. I've got a remnant. You're not the only one. Just keep on searching. Just keep on looking. They're out there."

THE WATCHMEN

Song of Solomon 3:3 (NASB)
The watchmen who make the rounds in the city found me, and I said, 'Have you seen him whom my soul loves?'

Now, the watchmen here are the elders of the church, the pastors and the spiritual leaders. Notice, first of all, that they found her. She was back inside the doors of the church, so to speak, so they greet her and ask, "Where have you been?" She doesn't have time to respond to their concerns, but immediately asks, "Have you seen him whom my soul loves? You're the elders, the leaders, the pastors... surely you can tell me where I can find Him."

Let's focus here for just a moment. There's a large group of Christians out there who've been hurt and offended by Christian leadership. But, you can't stay in that place of being offended if you want to rise up to the place God is calling you to. Personally, I had an awesome opportunity to be bitter and angry against Christian leadership after my ex-husband's affair, when I and my kids were asked to leave our church. But I couldn't stay in that place of offense. My relationship with the Lord was too important to harbor ill will and bitterness. Just like the Shulamite woman, I cried out, "Have you seen the One my soul loves? Do you know where He is?"

In verse 4, it says, "Scarcely had I passed them by...." She went right past the leaders. She didn't have time to chit-chat with them. She was searching for her lover, and they hadn't seen him so she continued in her search. She's saying, "Oh, you haven't seen Him? Okay then, I'm going to keep on looking for Him." Listen, don't let leaders stop you from finding Him. We put pastors and church leaders on pedestals, but they're human. They're not always able to help us.

Ultimately, our search for the Lord is our own. The pathway of intimacy is always individual. We can look to others for help but the responsibility of the search rests on our shoulders. When others can't help you, just keep on moving toward the Lord until you find Him. Did you notice the watchmen didn't answer her? They didn't tell her where He was. Some of them don't even know how to find Jesus themselves, much less help others with their pursuit of the Lord. So, remember, don't give up the search if Christian leaders cannot help you.

DON'T LET GO!

Song of Solomon 3:4 (NIV) Scarcely had I passed them when I found the one my heart loves. I held him and would not let him go till I had brought him to my mother's house, to the room of the one who conceived me.

The Passion Translation says, *"Then I encountered Him."* The word *encounter* means "to meet face-to-face." Yes, the world needs to *encounter* Him. But, it's not just the world that needs to meet Him face-to-face. The Body of Christ does, too.

When she found Him she said, "I held him and would not let him go...." Listen, when you find the Lord, when you get to the place where His presence is, you will not let that go. Nothing else will ever satisfy you again. You'll want more and more of Him. And, the more you experience of Him, and the more you encounter Him, the better representative you will be for Him to a world that desperately needs His presence. You see, we haven't been representing Him correctly, because we've been religious instead of being relational. We haven't been passionate, and on fire in love with Him. Revival comes when the church falls in love with Jesus!

So, she discovered that she could lose His presence and she said, "I'm never taking this for granted again." There are churches like that frog in the pot of boiling water. They don't realize they're slowly losing His presence. Some are already boiled... God's presence is no longer there and they haven't even missed it. Individuals can lose the presence of God. Churches can lose the presence of God. Even nations can lose the presence of God. But, "If my people who are called by My name...." God always starts with His people. Nations don't impact the church. No! The church is supposed to impact the nations. Stop blaming political parties for the trouble in our nation. It's a lack of Jesus Christ. The church has got to do a better job of representing Jesus to this nation. The world needs to see the church rising up to be the Bride of Christ. When they "taste and see" the good things of God's kingdom that we're experiencing, it will draw them to Him.

The first person I ever led to the Lord said, "What have you got? I want whatever it is." She thought I was on some kind of drug. She was willing to take any pill I gave her. She took the gos-pill!

HaHa! She swallowed it hook, line and sinker. She got on her knees, threw her hands in the air and got saved on the spot. I didn't even witness to her. I didn't have to read the book "Twenty Steps to Getting People Saved." I just sat in front of her and smiled, like a light. You couldn't take that smile off my face, because I'd had a face-to-face encounter with the Lord. I loved the Lord and it showed, so she thought I was high on something. She was a depressed, miserable person, but she saw something in me that she didn't have and she wanted it. It was easy to lead her to Christ. She saw *Him* in *me*.

So, there are a few things we can see in this story as it unfolds in chapter 3. First, the Shulamite woman discovered that she could lose his presence. The same can happen to us in our relationship with the Lord.

Secondly, in times of turmoil, when you realize you've lost His presence, it should birth a holy violence inside you. There should be something rise up in you that is a holy violence, kind of like when Jacob wrestled with God. "I'm not going to let you go until you bless me! I'm not going to let you go, Lord. If I have to be up all night, wrestling and praying and seeking and going to every place in town searching for you, I'm not going to give up. Yes, there should be something inside of you rise up with a desperate, holy violence. Why do I say that? Matthew 11:12 says, "The kingdom of God suffers violence and the violent take it by force." Take what by force? The kingdom of God! The lazy don't inherit the kingdom of God. Those who stay in their comfort zone don't find the kingdom. No. The violent find the kingdom.

THE VIOLENT BRIDE

I want to write another book called "The Violent Bride." I see a bride right now who is all beat up. She's weak-willed, wishy-washy, wimpy and not taking territory for the kingdom of God. She needs to rise up and take it by force. Her husband, Jesus

Christ, gave it to her. She should be a violent end-time bride. Don't get me wrong. I'm not talking about physically violent, with knives and guns and such. I'm talking about spiritually violent. A bride that says, "You're not getting in my way, devil. Prepare to be defeated!" Right now, the Body of Christ is so distracted with demonic ankle biters. We say, "The devil's been after me all day long and I don't know how to

get rid of him. I can't get him off of me." Violence is the answer. Forcible violence in the spirit realm, by a Bride who knows her authority through Jesus Christ. A Bride that's not afraid of a spiritual battle.

Think about a mother's love for a moment. I don't know a mama that would just sit by while her kid is being beaten up by the devil through drugs, alcohol, incest, or anything else abusive. She's not going to just sit back and say, "It's alright. I'll just stay in my prayer closet and pray." At least, none of the mamas that I know would do that. Listen, you can pray all you want to, but when you get done you better have a whip in your hand. "That's my baby! You better take your hands off of them right now, Satan!" That's how a righteous mama acts. When it comes to her kids she's ready to fight. That's what "*take it by force*" means. That's the kind of violent bride the end-time Bride of Christ is going to be.

The third thing we learn from the Shulamite woman from this passage is that it's not only *possible* to live without God's presence but you can actually learn how to *survive* without it. You can get so complacent, and so comfortable in dead religion, that you stay within the confines of your comfort zone, never reaching out for the greater things God has for you. The only way out of it will come through holy desperation, just like when Jacob said, "I will not let go of you until you bless me."

The fourth thing we see is that the Lord has bound Himself to our own passion. He obligates Himself to our passionate pursuit of Him. When the king withdrew his presence from the Shulamite woman, she pursued him until she found him. She left no stone unturned in her search for him. When he saw how she passionately pursued him, he came running. Likewise, when the Bride of Christ hungers and thirsts for God's presence, He says, "I will not deny her. I will not withhold My presence from her. I will pour myself out on her." He shows His overwhelming love for His bride.

CREATING HUNGER

How do you create hunger and thirst in the natural realm? You take food away to create hunger. You take drink away to create thirst. Right? How do you create hunger? You don't eat. Your stomach starts growling. You start feeling light-headed. The result is hunger.

Take that same understanding into the spiritual realm. How do you create spiritual hunger and thirst? God withdraws Himself. He's our source of spiritual food and drink. He is our spiritual nourishment. So He will create hunger in us simply by withdrawing His presence from us for a season of time in order to draw us closer to Him.

BRING JESUS TO CHURCH

Song of Solomon 3:4 (NIV)
I held him and would not let him go till I had brought him to my mother's house, to the room of the one who conceived me.

The *mother* in this scripture refers to the church. She was saying, "I'm not going to let Him go. I'm going to bring Him to the church." It speaks of the corporate Body of Christ... the family of God. Sometimes that's the most difficult place to bring Jesus to. Yes, sometimes it's actually difficult to bring Jesus to church!

Spiritually dull people, dry people, and spiritually complacent people oftentimes quench the fire of passionate believers. They say, "You don't really need to do all of that. You're being too 'over the top.' There's no need to be so outspoken and demonstrative in worship. You're calling too much attention to yourself." Many ministers and spiritual leaders warn their people to stay away from folks who are "too emotional" in their worship of the Lord. "I hear they're swinging from the chandeliers and rolling down the aisles over at that church. You need to stay away from those kind of people."

But, some understand the importance of passionate and fiery worship. I know of a pastor of a very large church who is not afraid of passionate worship in his congregation of 5,000 people. He says, "I'd rather pull them off the ceiling than have to raise them from the dead."

FROM THE INTIMATE TO THE CORPORATE

So, what she is saying is, "I'm going to bring this relationship that I have with Jesus to His Church, because He loves His Church. I will bring the revelation of my King to other believers who are desperate for His presence." She's determined to bring Him to her close relationships, too. Now, it can be difficult sometimes to share Him with your family and friends, because they know you intimately. But she's saying, "I'm not ashamed. I am His and He is mine. He's a part of me and I will show who He is to everyone I meet, everywhere I go. I will not be embarrassed. I will not be ashamed. I want to create a hunger inside of you. I hope my passion causes you to realize there's more."

In verse 4 of chapter 1, Jesus brought her into His chambers, but now she's bringing Him into the Church. That's the way it works. You go from the intimate place to the corporate place. If you don't have Him in His chambers you can't bring Him to the corporate Church. She's now confident in who she is. She's Jesus' Bride. She's confident in her assignment with Him, that she's called to the nations with Him. It's a new season. She found the one her soul loves. It is springtime and the night and the winter has passed.

A "DO NOT DISTURB" SIGN

Now, in verse 5, the king comes in. She's hanging on to him, not willing to let him go. All of the onlookers are seeing this. The critical family members, the naysayers, the friends. She's telling all of them, "I'm not letting go of him." So, the king rises up and responds. He's talking to the daughters of Jerusalem when he says:

Song of Solomon 3:5 (NKJV)
I charge you, O daughters of Jerusalem, by the gazelles or by the does of the field, do not stir up nor awaken love until it pleases.

Remember, the daughters of Jerusalem prophetically represent the onlookers in your life who are watching your relationship with the Lord. They're the aunts and uncles, the grandmas and grandpas, the in-laws and the outlaws, and the naysayers in your life. He's telling them once again, just like he did in chapter 2, and just like he will again in chapter 8... He's saying three times, "Don't interfere with what I'm doing in the life of My Bride." For the immature believers, for the carnal Christians and for the unbelievers who lack discernment of what God is doing, He hangs over His Bride a sign that says "Do Not Disturb." He's telling them, "Leave My Bride alone. I'm doing something in her, and even though you may not see it now, or understand it, I'm doing a work in her. I'm raising up an end-time Bride who knows who I am and knows the authority I've given her."

If you've encountered the Lord, then you're called to bring Him to the Church, to the Corporate Body of Christ. The Church needs to see that it's a living mutual relationship. He passionately pursues you, and you passionately pursue Him as well. Many people go to church out of duty and obligation. They don't expect to encounter God when they come. But, when we come together to worship, God has promised to inhabit the praises of His people. Where there's no praise, there's no presence. And, where there's no presence, there's no joy, because the scripture says, "In His presence is fullness of joy." So, if you're going to a church where there is no joy, it's because there's no presence. And the reason there's no presence is because there's no praise. There's nothing coming from that place of an intimate exchange. There's no love affair. It's just duty and obligation and a token song, but no actual worship.

So we're receiving a charge from the King to leave His Bride alone, as He prepares her for this final hour. What is all this preparation leading to? You'll find out in the next chapter.

CHAPTER 8
THE ROYAL WEDDING

In this chapter, we're going to look at the royal wedding. Our focus will be on Chapter 3 of the Song of Solomon, verses 6-11. These six verses will revolutionize your life. They'll revolutionize your walk with the Lord and change the way you serve Him. They'll change your outlook in your prayers, and in your purpose, because you'll begin to see *who* you are, and *whose* you are and *where* you're going.

Now, usually, when we think of royal weddings, we think of Great Britain and the English monarchy. We think of Prince Charles marrying Diana, or Prince William marrying Kate. The latest royal wedding was Prince Harry and Meghan Markle. Hundreds of millions of people throughout the world turned on their television sets to watch these historic weddings. Some people even traveled across the ocean to see these weddings firsthand.

But the royal wedding we're talking about is going to be the most regal, the most royal, the most majestic, the most glorious royal wedding that has ever taken place. And it won't just be viewed by hundreds of millions of people watching via television. The Bible says that this royal wedding will be seen by every eye. It will be seen by every person who has ever lived upon this Earth, from the first man Adam, to the last person who will be born on planet Earth. Some will see it from afar, while others will see it up close. The Bible says, "Blessed are those who are invited to the wedding supper of the Lamb." Those are the people who accepted the invitation. Those who have made Jesus their Lord are on the guest list!

I shared with you earlier that a time is coming in Song of Solomon where it will be written, "Who is this coming up out of the wilderness leaning on her beloved?" I can't wait to get to that verse so we can expound on it, because that represents the Bride of Christ rising up out of the wilderness. But, before she comes out, I want you to see this in verses 6-11 of chapter 3.

Song of Solomon 3:6-11 (NIV)
6 Who is this coming up from the wilderness like a column of smoke, perfumed with myrrh and incense made from all the spices of the merchant?
7 Look! It is Solomon's carriage, escorted by sixty warriors, the noblest of Israel,
8 all of them wearing the sword, all experienced in battle, each with his sword at his side, prepared for the terrors of the night.
9 King Solomon made for himself the carriage; he made it of wood from Lebanon.
10 Its posts he made of silver, its base of gold. Its seat was upholstered with purple, its interior inlaid with love. Daughters of Jerusalem,
11 come out, and look, you daughters of Zion. Look on King Solomon wearing a crown, the crown with which his mother crowned him on the day of his wedding, the day his heart rejoiced.

I bring this message with fear and trepidation because I know the weight of the message I'm bringing. This is truly the end-time message. This truly is where we are going. This is what is going to happen. I can't give you this revelation. I can't make you understand it, nor can I make you rise up to take hold of this message.

So, I pray that the Holy Spirit brings you the revelation of what I'm about to say, because with the revelation comes the awakening.

The end-time revival, the end-time harvest, the end-time awakening, comes with this revelation. He's not coming back for a *church*. He's coming back for a *glorious Bride*, and until we become that, until we step into our destiny, we're holding Him back.

A WARRIOR BRIDE

The book of Song of Solomon is an end-time prophecy, just like the book of Revelation. It is an end-time prophecy of things that will transpire... things that will take place in the future. It is a love song from King Solomon to the Shulamite woman. It is a love song from King Jesus to His end-time Bride. Song of Solomon goes hand-in-hand with the book of Revelation. The book of Revelation puts fear in people. People are afraid of that book. They're afraid of what's coming. There's fear connected with the end times. But, the Bible tells us that perfect love casts out fear. So, doesn't it stand to reason that a God of perfect love would combine the book of Revelation with the Song of Solomon? This end-time Bride will not fear! She will be confident; she will be secure and bold. She'll be a warrior Bride.

Why does this warrior Bride teach about warfare? Because she knows who she is. She knows who she represents. Listen, you'll fight for something you love. You'll go to war for somebody you love. You don't fight for something you don't believe in. But, when you're passionate for your country, for your family, for your homeland, you'll fight. All the great movies that people love, like "Braveheart" for instance, are love stories about men who went to war to fight for the women. "The Passion of the Christ" was the greatest love story of all time, and it's one of the most violent movies you'll ever see. It's a story of war, and of redemption. Best of all, it's a true story! It's a story about the Son of God going to war for His Bride.

THE WILDERNESS

So, we're looking at Song of Solomon 3:6 and it starts off with, "Who is this?" It starts off with a question, and it's a question every one of us will have to answer. Both the saved and the unsaved. Everyone is going to have to answer the question, "Who is this coming up for the desert." The New King James says it this way, "Who is this coming out of the wilderness?" Out of the wilderness. Let's focus here for a moment.

If you recall, I mentioned in an earlier chapter how God spoke, through the prophet Hosea, "I will allure her, will bring her into the wilderness, and speak comfort to her." He allured her into a private place. It was not a place of punishment. Many times, when the Body of Christ hears the word *wilderness* we think, "I'm going to go through hell. The wilderness isn't a good place. I'd rather be on the mountaintop." Isn't that the truth? But, we learn that the wilderness isn't a place of punishment. No! It's a place of privacy, where God can take her (His Bride) away from the distractions and disruptions of life. It's in the wilderness where God promises to give her back her vineyard. If God is leading you into the wilderness, it is to restore you. "He leads me beside still waters. He restores my soul." Let's look again at that passage from Hosea 2:

Hosea 2:14-15 (NKJV)
14 "Therefore, behold, I will allure her, will bring her into the wilderness, and speak comfort to her.
15 I will give her her vineyards from there, and the Valley of Achor as a door of hope; She shall sing there, as in the days of her youth, as in the day when she came up from the land of Egypt.

The word Achor means "trouble." So God has promised to turn our valley of trouble into a door of hope. When God takes you into that secret place to restore your soul, and to bring you into that close, intimate place the scripture says you're going to sing like the days of your youth. You're going to sing like the day you first got saved... when He first took you out of the slavery of Egypt so He could bring you to the Promised Land. Egypt represents the world, and your flesh, and your sin. He says you're going to sing like the day you first gave your life to me. And, when that song rises up in your heart, verse 16 goes on to say:

Hosea 2:16 (NKJV)
"And it shall be, in that day," says the Lord, "That you will call Me 'My Husband,' and no longer call Me 'My Master,'

Isn't it awesome how one scripture backs up another scripture? Hosea backs up Song of Solomon. God's prophesying to His people, "When I bring you up out of this place you're going to have the revelation that I am your husband, and you are my wife. The literal translation of that word "wilderness" is the word "mouth." The wilderness is where God speaks to us. Your greatest revelation of who you are and who your husband is will come out of that place. It will come when you are in the wilderness.

So, now we can answer the question, "Who is this coming up out of the wilderness?" It's King Solomon leading the Shulamite woman out of the wilderness... showing her the way out. It's God, bringing the Bride of Christ out of the wilderness after He's revealed to her that He is her husband.

LIKE A COLUMN OF SMOKE

Song of Solomon 3:6 says, "Like a column of smoke" he is coming up out of the wilderness. That column of smoke was from the burning incense in King Solomon's procession. In the Bible, smoke speaks of the glory cloud. It speaks of the glory of God. In 2 Chronicles 5:14 it says the priests could not perform their service because a cloud filled the house of God. It goes on to say that the glory of the Lord was in that cloud.

So, what we're seeing here is Solomon's wedding procession coming up out of the wilderness, and he's coming in a glory cloud. He is coming with the incense of the procession burning all around him. Exodus 13:21 says, "By day the Lord went ahead of them in a pillar of cloud to guide them on their way." This happened while the children of Israel were in the wilderness. So this column of smoke is indicative of the guiding cloud in the wilderness that led the children of Israel, and it also represents the smoke of the altar of incense... the glory of God.

The royal wedding procession is coming out of the wilderness because that is where you meet Him and get the fullest revelation of how much He loves you. Before you went into the wilderness, you were questioning God. But, while you were in the wilderness, you learned about His faithfulness. You came to understand that He is not only faithful on the mountaintops but also in the wilderness. Take a look at what Revelation 19:6-10 says:

Revelation 19:6-10 (NIV)
6 Then I heard what sounded like a great multitude, like the roar of rushing waters and like loud peals of thunder, shouting: "Hallelujah! For our Lord God Almighty reigns.
7 Let us rejoice and be glad and give him glory! For the wedding of the Lamb has come, and his bride has made herself ready.
8 Fine linen, bright and clean, was given her to wear."(Fine linen stands for the righteous acts of God's holy people.)
9 Then the angel said to me, "Write this: Blessed are those who are invited to the wedding supper of the Lamb!" And he added, "These are the true words of God."
10 At this I fell at his feet to worship him. But he said to me, "Don't do that! I am a fellow servant with you and with your brothers and sisters who hold to the testimony of Jesus. Worship God! For it is the Spirit of prophecy who bears testimony to Jesus."

WEDDING GARMENTS

Take note of verse 8 where it says "Fine linen, bright and clean...." If you feel dirty and dull you haven't gotten your bridal garments on yet. When the Shulamite woman said, "I am dark," it was obvious she hadn't received her "bright and clean" wedding garments yet. God wants to change your wardrobe. He wants to put bridal garments on you. If you still look at yourself as "dark" then you're not seeing yourself, and identifying yourself, as the end-time Bride. Verse 8 goes on to define what the fine linen is symbolic of... "Fine linen stands for the righteous acts of God's holy people."

The angel tells John to write this down: "Blessed are those who are invited to the wedding supper of the Lamb." You have been given an invitation, but it's not just to come and spectate. You see, it's not just an invitation *to* a wedding. It's an invitation *to be* His Bride. And those who reply with "Yes" to this invitation receive a blessing. He said, "*Blessed* are those who are invited...." Then he added, "These are the true words of God."

In verse 10 the angel reminds John that "It is the Spirit of prophecy who bears testimony of Jesus." Both end-time prophetic books, Revelation and Song of Solomon, bear testimony to Jesus, because the Spirit of prophecy is on them.

MYRRH AND INCENSE

Song of Solomon 3:6-11 (NIV)
6 Who is this coming up from the wilderness like a column of smoke, perfumed with myrrh and incense made from all the spices of the merchant?

Notice that He is *perfumed* with myrrh and incense made from all the spices of the merchant. Myrrh was a spice that was used in the burial of the dead. "He was perfumed with myrrh." Jesus came for His Bride *perfumed* to sacrifice His life for her. The fragrance of myrrh was all over Jesus. It represents the fragrance of His suffering and His finished work at the cross. It speaks of His death to purchase His Bride. Now, it doesn't say, "He was reeking of myrrh." The smell of myrrh is a beautiful aroma, and it is pleasing to the nostrils of God. The smell of myrrh at Jesus' burial was the payment for the Bride of Christ. He purchased His Bride through His suffering, by laying down His life for her.

Ephesians 5:25 (NIV)
Husbands, love your wives, just as Christ loved the church and gave himself up for her.

How did Jesus show how much He loved His Bride? He laid His life down for her. He gave Himself up for her. So, He was perfumed in myrrh on that cross, just as Solomon was also perfumed with it when He came out of the wilderness.

He was also perfumed with incense, which is frankincense. Frankincense represents intercession. Jesus not only interceded on the cross for all mankind, but as He hung upon that cross, the act itself was an act of intercession. The word *intercession* means "to stand in the gap between Heaven and Earth, between God and man." When Jesus hung upon that cross, He was suspended in the air, between Heaven and Earth... between God and man. That cross represented Christ's intercession and, according to Hebrews 7:25, the blood of the cross still intercedes today.

Hebrews 7:25 (NIV)
Therefore he is able to save completely those who come to God through him, because he always lives to intercede for them.

Always! He is seated at the right hand of the Father interceding. If you look at the book of Job, Satan comes before the throne of God accusing Job, pointing at him, saying, "He's only serving You because You're blessing him." That's what Satan does, day and night. He's called "the accuser of the brethren." It's his job to accuse you before God, and he's good at it. So, when you feel beat up all week, just realize where it's coming from. But, Jesus is sitting at the right hand of the Father, forever making intercession for us. All of the accusations Satan makes against us can't be seen because the blood of Jesus covers us. God says, "I don't see it. I can't see what you're saying, Satan." Christ's intercession for us covers us. That's what the incense in this wedding procession symbolizes.

THE MERCHANT

Now, what is the meaning of "the merchant" in this verse? Let's look at Matthew 13:44-46 to help answer that question.

Matthew 13:44-46 (NIV)
44 "The kingdom of heaven is like treasure hidden in a field. When a man found it, he hid it again, and then in his joy went and sold all he had and bought that field.
45 "Again, the kingdom of heaven is like a merchant looking for fine pearls.
46 When he found one of great value, he went away and sold everything he had and bought it.

In these verses, Jesus is comparing the kingdom of Heaven to a merchant. He said this merchant was looking for fine pearls. When he found one of great value, he sold all he had so he could buy it. That merchant was Jesus. He was perfumed in myrrh and incense, and those spices were brought by the merchants of the Middle East. Those particular spices could only be found in one place – the Arabian Desert. So, they were particularly expensive to purchase. Myrrh did not grow like weeds in a garden. You had to go into the desert, into the wilderness, to find it. That's what Jesus did. There was a high price He paid for those spices. Jesus gave everything he had so He could purchase us as His Bride.

SIXTY NOBLE WARRIORS

Song of Solomon 3:7-8 (NIV)
7 Look! It is Solomon's carriage, escorted by sixty warriors, the noblest of Israel,
8 all of them wearing the sword, all experienced in battle, each with his sword at his side, prepared for the terrors of the night.

There's a lot in this passage. The first thing I want us to look at is Solomon's carriage. What is Solomon's carriage? It's a wedding coach. It's a traveling throne. In the eastern world, on her wedding day, a bride was carried on men's shoulders throughout the streets in a sedan chair that was referred to as a coach. In the passage above, we find Solomon sitting in this wedding carriage, being carried up to his bride. What we're seeing here is the bridal procession. This is symbolic of the Lord coming to meet the Bride of Christ.

He is escorted by sixty warriors. He's not coming alone. These warriors surrounding the throne speaks of God's extravagant protection. By the way, there were sixty support pillars in Moses' tabernacle. This passage says that these sixty warriors were the most noble men of Israel. They were men who would lay down their lives to protect the King and his bride.

I want you to notice that the closest people to the King were warriors. The closest ones bringing the King to meet his bride in this royal procession were the warriors. You won't find the weak, the feeble, the wishy-washy, the double-minded, the lukewarm protecting the King and his bride. No! You're going to find the strongest, the most noble of Israel. All of them were wearing the sword. All were experienced in battle. Some Christians say, "I don't like all this talk about spiritual warfare." Listen, you'll never learn *how* to war if you don't ever *go* to war. You don't get experience in war sitting on the sidelines.

The Royal Wedding

The Bible says in Judges 3:1-2 that God left certain nations in the land of Canaan to test Israel, because there was a whole generation of young Israelites who had no experience in war. He said, "I'm leaving them there so they can learn how to war." This is part of my personal end-time assignment, to train the next generation on how to war in the Spirit. This nation needs to learn how to win a war. We haven't won a war since World War 2. The greatest military minds that have ever lived in America are dying off. Now we have a breed, a generation, that doesn't like war and doesn't understand there is a need for it at times. This mindset has crept over into the Body of Christ, and I combat it day and night. My God trains my hands for war and my fingers for battle. My God is a warrior. He's a Warrior King.

THINK LIKE A WARRIOR

Listen, I love God's grace and I know I wouldn't be here today without it, but there's such a greasy grace teaching out there that says you don't have to war because the battle is over. But, if that was the case, everyone would be saved and all the churches would be packed. Yes, the battle for salvation was won by Jesus Christ when He said, "It is finished," but Ephesians reminds us that "we wrestle not against flesh and blood, but against principalities, against powers, against rulers of the darkness of this world...." Don't get caught up in doctrine that makes the church weak, and that doesn't have weapons, or armor, or a warfare mode and mindset. The church has gotten beaten up, and has failed to advance against the kingdom of darkness because we don't have a warfare mindset. The ones who were closest to the king were the ones who wore their swords, all experienced in battle, prepared for the terrors of night. They were the prepared ones. They were the mature ones. Their swords were strapped to their thighs, just like the gunfighters in the old western movies.

You don't go to war without your weapon! These guys were "locked and loaded." They were ready to go at all times. You don't wait until someone breaks into your house to go looking for your gun. No! You keep your weapon nearby. Jesus told the disciples, "Watch and pray." You pray, and you keep one eye open. "I'm watching you, devil. You're not coming in during the night watch. If you try to attack me in the middle of the night, you better watch out, because I keep my weapon right by my bed every night." My Bible, the sword of the Spirit, stays right beside my bed on my nightstand. If he tries to attack me I just start reading God's Word. If he's trying to steal my sleep at night, I just open up my Bible, and fill my spirit with ammunition from God's Word. He'll regret attacking me in the night hour! Think like a warrior. Think like a soldier!

The image of these warriors wearing their swords brings to mind the book of Nehemiah, when the Israelites were rebuilding the wall that surrounded their city. The wall was originally built to protect the city and to keep invaders out, but there were breaches in the wall that left the city susceptible to invasion. The Israelites were rebuilding the wall and repairing the breaches, but their enemies were threatening to stop them. They mocked the builders and tried their best to discourage them.

Nehemiah 4:17-18 (NIV)
17 ... Those who carried materials did their work with one hand and held a weapon in the other, 18 and each of the builders wore his sword at his side as he worked. But the man who sounded the trumpet stayed with me.

That's a picture of the army of Christ. They were prepared for the terrors of the night. They were ready for nighttime attacks. They weren't afraid of the dark or of the enemy. They were prepared for whatever might happen. They always had their sword by their side.

Psalm 91:5 (NIV)
You will not fear the terror of night, nor the arrow that flies by day....

The Royal Wedding

No! We don't fear, because perfect love has cast out fear. I'm passionately in love with my King and I'm ready to fight for Him.

I know what it's like to go to battle. I've warred for my son when he was out on drugs and almost killing himself. I was wrestling for him in prayer. I was wielding the sword of the Spirit on his behalf. I had the mindset of a warrior. That's what the end-time Bride of Christ needs to have... a warrior mentality.

THE MARRIAGE CARRIAGE

Song of Solomon 3:9 (NIV)
King Solomon made for Himself the carriage;

The scripture says that King Solomon built this marriage coach (marriage bed) for himself. It's a traveling throne and he made it with his own hands. There is an interesting parallel here when we understand that King Solomon is representative of Jesus Christ. What was Jesus' profession when He was on Earth? He was a carpenter! Can you see the beautiful parallels in this story and the gospel story? Christ Himself has prepared a marriage bed for His Bride.

The Bible says that God prepares a table before you in the presence of your enemies. He brings you to the table that He built for you, but that isn't the end. There's a royal wedding carriage that He has built so He can carry you as His beloved Bride.

When you watch royal weddings over in Great Britain, they always come in on a beautiful wedding carriage. Those carriages pale in comparison to the one being built for the Bride of Christ. Now, the carriage that Solomon hand-crafted was made from the cedars of Lebanon. This wood was the strongest, most fragrant wood in all the land of Israel. An interesting fact about the cedar of Lebanon is that it doesn't rot like other trees in the forest. This wood doesn't decay. Also, it was a very expensive wood. The wedding carriage that Jesus made for His Bride cost Him everything, and it will never decay... it is everlasting!

BUILT IN THE WILDERNESS

The carriage was built in the wilderness. King Solomon built it for the Shulamite woman when he was in the wilderness with her, where he drew her to himself away from all the distractions and disruptions of life. Likewise, Jesus drew you away to that private place in the wilderness. He called you away from the distractions that had pulled you away from His presence. In the wilderness you drew closer to Him. In the wilderness He tested you to see if you would follow Him all the way. In the wilderness He asked you what He asked Peter, "Do you love Me more than these? Will you love Me when everyone else is running away from Me?"

He's asking His Bride, "Do you really love me? Will you stay with me no matter what, even if you never feel another Holy Ghost goose bump again? Even if I don't bless you with another thing for the rest of your life, will I still be your King? Will I still be your Lord? Will you still serve Me? Will you still love Me?" Yes, it's in that wilderness where He deals with your flesh nature, that part of you that fights against Him. He's killing that old nature inside of you that's resistant to His Lordship, while He's asking you, "Will you love Me? Will you be there for Me? Can I trust you? Can I trust you with the things I'm about to bless you with? Can I trust you with all I'm about to do in your life? Can I trust you with My Glory?" All the while, He's carving a marriage bed for Himself and for His Bride.

This is where we are today as the Bride of Christ. The Bride is almost prepared for the arrival of the wedding procession, and the closer we get to the time of Christ's return, the closer and stronger His presence is going to be.

Now, verse 10 describes this marriage carriage in detail.

Song of Solomon 3:10 (NIV)
Its posts he made of silver, its base of gold. Its seat was upholstered with purple, its interior [lovingly] inlaid with love. [by the] Daughters of Jerusalem,.

Silver speaks of redemption. So, it's saying the posts of this marriage are made in redemption. Posts are a symbol of strength, stability and steadfastness. Posts are what hold up and supports a structure or monument. So, the strength and stability of your life as the Bride of Christ is found in your redemption.

The base of the marriage bed was made of gold. What is the base? It's the foundation of this marriage. The foundation of this marriage union is gold. Gold speaks of divinity. It speaks of the divine character and glory of God. So, this marriage bed is held up and supported by your redemption and it rests upon the foundation of God's character, nature and glory.

SEATED WITH HIM IN HEAVENLY PLACES

The seat was upholstered in purple. You probably already know that the color purple represents royalty. This is a royal seat the King is about to sit His Bride upon.

Ephesians 2:6 reminds us that God has "seated us with Him in Heavenly places in Christ Jesus." As the Bride of Christ, He has given us a royal seat, on a royal throne, in a royal place. We're seated right next to Him on the royal throne, because we are His Bride. Can you see how this reference from Song of Solomon is corroborated in Ephesians 2:6?

Now, the best part about this throne, this marriage carriage that He is building for His Bride, is that the interior was lovingly inlaid *with love*. The innermost part of this marriage bed is paved with God's perfect, complete love. I often hear Christians say, "I don't know if God loves me." People wrestle with that thought when they get saved. "Do you really love me God? How could you love me? My life has been such a mess!" But, when they find out who they are, His purchased Bride, the doubts about His love for them disintegrates.

If you're still looking at your old sinful nature and identifying with "the old you," you're not seeing the person God called you to be and created you to be. But, when you see the great price He paid to purchase you as His Bride, then you begin to understand your true value and worth. When you see how much He loved you, it changes the way you look at yourself.

Now, notice what the last part of verse 10 says. "It's interior [lovingly] inlaid [by the] daughters of Jerusalem. A better translation of that phrase is *"for* the daughters of Jerusalem." The Passion Translation states it this way: "The king himself has made it for those who will become his bride...." He made the marriage bed for those who *will* (in the future) become His Bride.

COME OUT AND LOOK

Song of Solomon 3:11 (NIV)
Come out, and look, you daughters of Zion. Look on King Solomon wearing a crown, the crown with which his mother crowned him on the day of his wedding, the day his heart rejoiced.

Now, in the first chapter of this book I mentioned that the daughters of Jerusalem represent the onlookers in your life – those who are watching you, who haven't yet received the full revelation of the end-time Bride. They might be in the church, and they might be saved, they might be baby Christians, but they haven't received the revelation of who God is, and who they are in relation to Him. She's saying, "*Come out* of your religion. *Come out* of your tradition. *Come out* of your wrong mindsets. *Come out* of your old ways, and your old wineskins." She's saying to them, "*Look* at Him. *Look* at King Jesus. *Look* at the crown on His head.

Come out and look at the King wearing the crown. Behold your King!" She wants them to get the same revelation she has.

When you meet Him you can't help but want to share Him and bring others to Him. I can't do dead church anymore. I can't do religion anymore. I can't do that old tradition anymore. I'm never going back. I've met the King in all His Glory and all His Splendor. I am passionately in love with Him, so if you want to try and box Him in and box in my worship I can't do that anymore. He's coming back for a glorious Bride. He's coming back for a Church who loves Him with reckless abandon. She's saying, "Feast your eyes on this king, O' brides to be, all of you who are going to come into the kingdom."

At my home church we've been praying for our nation. We've been praying that the church will wake up. We've been praying that Prince Charming, the Prince of Peace, will come kiss Sleeping Beauty and wake her up. As the church goes, so goes the nation.

THE CROWN UPON HIS HEAD

Song of Solomon 3:11 mentions the crown upon his head. Revelation 19:12 adds further details:

Revelation 19:12 (NIV)
His eyes are like blazing fire, and on his head are many crowns.

Many crowns! There's not just one crown on His head. The book of Revelation says there are many crowns on His head. It goes on to say that He has a name written on Him that no one knows but Himself. He's the King of all kings. He's the Lord of all lords. He's the Sovereign Authority over all of Heaven and all of Earth. He's the King over Heaven. He's the King over the angels. He's the King over the Earth. He's the King over the Church. He's the King throughout eternity. On His head are many crowns!

Song of Solomon 3:11 (NIV)
... the crown with which his mother crowned him on the day of his wedding, the day his heart rejoiced.

PROVERBS 31 WOMAN - THE BRIDE OF CHRIST

Now, Bathsheba was Solomon's mother. She is the mother being referred to in the scripture verse above. An interesting side note here is that Proverbs 31 is written by King Solomon (who is referred to as King Lemuel in the passage). Proverbs 31:1 says, "The sayings of King Lemuel–an inspired utterance his mother taught him." When we put all of this information together we come to understand that "The Virtuous Woman" of Proverbs 31 was actually written by Bathsheba. Or, it would be more accurate to say that it originated with Bathsheba, and was penned by her son, Solomon. How can this be? Wasn't she an adulteress? Didn't she commit adultery with King David? Wasn't she guilty of her husband Uriah's death, just as much as King David was? That's right! After Bathsheba repented of her adultery, and God gave her a second chance, she was able to present her son with an illustration of the kind of virtuous woman he should be looking for as his wife. Proverbs 31 gives the perfect description of the end-time Bride of Christ, as well. It is written by a king whose mother taught him that God is God of the second chance. Yes, she did many things wrong, but she was able to tell Solomon, "I did things the wrong way, but let me tell you the right way." Praise God!

So, when you read Proverbs 31 starting with verse 10, you get a picture of what the Bride of Christ should look like.

Proverbs 31:10-12 (NIV)
10 A wife of noble character who can find? She is worth far more than rubies.
11 Her husband has full confidence in her and lacks nothing of value.
12 She brings him good, not harm, all the days of her life.

The Royal Wedding

When you read "She is worth far more than rubies," that's referring to the end-time Bride. Her husband (Jesus Christ) has full confidence in her and lacks nothing of value. What a different perspective on the Body of Christ! "She brings Him good, not harm, all the days of her life." That's the Bride! Can you see it? The Proverbs 31 woman is the Bride of Christ. She is clothed with strength and dignity. She can laugh at the days to come. She's fearless. She's a warrior. She speaks with wisdom, and faithful instruction is on her tongue. This is God's end-time Bride, the perfect wife that He's returning for.

This is who we are. It's not the letter of the law. If you hate Proverbs 31 because the woman depicted seems so far beyond the reach of what any woman can be, then you're reading it as "the letter of the law," and not seeing it in the Spirit. It's not referring to an individual. It's pointing to the future Bride of Christ. In the New International Version of the Bible, verse 10 is translated, "A wife of noble character who can find?" That word *noble* means "capable, intelligent." Did you get that? She's intelligent. Sometimes the church looks so stupid to the world. But, that's not the case. She's noble, capable, intelligent. Read Proverbs 31 again, but this time think about the woman as being the Bride of Christ and her husband is Jesus Christ. Proverbs 31 will take on a brand new meaning for you.

WE CROWN HIM AS KING!

Let's look at one more thing about the "crown with which his mother crowned him...."

Prophetically speaking, the mother being talked about here is referring to the church. The church crowns Jesus as King on His wedding day. The church will crown Him as King every time she surrenders to His love. In Revelation 14:14, Jesus is seen seated on a cloud wearing a crown of gold on His head, and a sickle in His hand. It depicts the end-time harvest. That crown, and the end-time harvest, and the Bride of Christ all go hand-in-hand. Let's look closer at Revelation 14:14-15.

Revelation 14:14-15 (NIV)
14 I looked, and there before me was a white cloud, and seated on the cloud was one like a son of man with a crown of gold on his head and a sharp sickle in his hand.
15 Then another angel came out of the temple and called in a loud voice to him who was sitting on the cloud, "Take your sickle and reap, because the time to reap has come, for the harvest of the earth is ripe."

He will wear that crown at the end-time harvest. Why do we say the end-time harvest will be the largest ingathering of souls? Because of the scripture we just read. That crown was placed on His head by the church as the wedding day approaches.

Now, there is one other crown that Jesus wore while He was here on Earth. Do you remember it? The crown of thorns. That crown was placed on His head to mock Him. That was the devil's doing. That crown wasn't placed on His head in honor. But, he endured the cross and wore that crown of thorns so He could purchase the Church, His Bride. He knew all along that one day He would be crowned with the crown He was deserving of. That crown of thorns pressed into His brow was a temporary mockery of His kingship, but the golden crown of honor, placed upon His head by the Church, will forever remain upon His head. Your King is waiting for you to crown Him.

Song of Solomon 3:11 (NIV)
... the crown with which his mother crowned him on the day of his wedding, the day his heart rejoiced.

"The day his heart rejoiced," in this passage, is referring to his wedding day. Do you understand that when Christ is finally united with His Bride it will bring Him great joy? That wedding day is not very far off! You've wondered, "Does God love me? Do I make Him happy? Do I put a smile on His face?" On His wedding day, all of your questions will be forever answered. His heart will rejoice on that day. You will see the joy on His face and will know for sure how much He loves you. You're His Bride.

Revelation 19 tells us that the twenty-four elders and the four living creatures fell down and worshipped Him who sat upon the throne as a proclamation was made, "Let us rejoice and be glad and give him glory! For the wedding of the Lamb has come, and his bride has made herself ready." (Revelation 19:7 - New International Version). After that, we read that the heavens will be opened and Jesus will be seen sitting on a white horse and, "on his head are many crowns." Can you see the correlation? Right before the Marriage Supper of the Lamb, Jesus is seen wearing the crowns. Can you see how Song of Solomon and Revelation tie together?

There's going to be a wedding... and YOU are the bride! I don't know how to make it any clearer. You are the Bride, and His heart will rejoice on His wedding day.

Isaiah 62:5 (NIV)
... as a bridegroom rejoices over his bride, so will your God rejoice over you.

God rejoices over getting you as His Bride!

Zephaniah 3:17 (NKJV)
The Lord your God in your midst, The Mighty One, will save; He will rejoice over you with gladness, He will quiet you with His love,.

Did you catch that? He will quiet you with His love. There are so many voices of agitation and discontentment in our world today. Politicians, media, democrats, republicans... everybody is going nuts! It's easy to become disquieted with all of the fuss going on around us. But, He will quiet us with this revelation... "You are mine. I love you."

CHAPTER 9

THE JEWISH WEDDING CEREMONY

John 14:1-3 (NIV)
1 Do not let your hearts be troubled. You believe in God; believe also in me.
2 My Father's house has many rooms; if that were not so, would I have told you that I am going there to prepare a place for you?
3 And if I go and prepare a place for you, I will come back and take you to be with me that you also may be where I am.

When we read this scripture we get a picture in our minds of Christ building a mansion for us, but we don't fully grasp that this is bridal language Jesus is using. Especially in modern America, we miss out on a lot of the beautiful marriage symbolism throughout the scriptures because the Jewish customs of the Old and New Testament are so foreign to us. So, I am going to weave both Old and New Testament passages together in this final chapter to describe how God, through Christ (our Bridegroom) is in the process of marrying His Bride, the Church (that's you and me). Now, I'm not going to be able to share all of the scriptures that pertain to this topic because there are hundreds of passages that refer to us as the Bride of Christ, or that talk about how the

Lord will be coming back for His Bride. But, I will share several scriptures that are centered around this thought of the Lord being our Bridegroom, and us being His Bride.

BRIDAL LANGUAGE IN THE OLD TESTAMENT

I'll start with a familiar passage in Isaiah 61.

Isaiah 61:1-3 (NIV)
1 The Spirit of the Sovereign Lord is on me, because the Lord has anointed me to proclaim good news to the poor. He has sent me to bind up the brokenhearted, to proclaim freedom for the captives and release from darkness for the prisoners,
2 to proclaim the year of the Lord's favor and the day of vengeance of our God, to comfort all who mourn,
3 and provide for those who grieve in Zion—to bestow on them a crown of beauty instead of ashes, the oil of joy instead of mourning, and a garment of praise instead of a spirit of despair.

You probably recognize this verse as being the passage from which Jesus read when He stood up in the synagogue to read in His hometown. After reading this passage, He said, "This day this Scripture is being fulfilled in your hearing." Believe it or not, this passage is a picture of Jesus' ministry in relationship to His Bride. When we read the first parts of this passage we often think of the ministry assignment Jesus has given us, to preach good news to the poor, to heal broken hearts, and to proclaim liberty to the captives. Rightly we should. But in verse 3 it says He's giving us a "crown of beauty instead of ashes, ... and a garment of praise." The "crown of beauty" that He's referring to is also called a "garland" in the New American Standard Version of the Bible. This garland is a bridal headpiece. So, He's giving us a bridal headpiece to replace the ashes of mourning. He's giving us a bridal identity. It goes on to say that He's giving us "garments of praise" for the spirit of heaviness. What are we wearing? Are we still sitting in sackcloth and ashes, constantly reminding ourselves of our old sin nature? Or, are we wearing the bridal headpiece He's placed on our heads with the beautiful robes of salvation He has furnished us with?

In Isaiah 62:3, we find similar terminology to Isaiah 61:3.

Isaiah 62:3 (NIV)
You will be a crown of splendor in the Lord's hand, a royal diadem in the hand of your God.

God is fashioning His people into a royal crown. He's fashioning us into a bridal headpiece... a headpiece of beauty. Isaiah 62:4-5 goes on to say:

HE'S GIVEN US A NEW NAME

Isaiah 62:4-5 (NKJV)
4 You shall no longer be termed Forsaken, nor shall your land any more be termed Desolate; but you shall be called Hephzibah, and your land Beulah; for the Lord delights in you, and your land shall be married.
5 For as a young man marries a virgin, so shall your sons marry you; and as the bridegroom rejoices over the bride, so shall your God rejoice over you.

So, not only is God fashioning us, the Bride of Christ, into a headpiece of beauty, He's also giving us a new name. Do you hear the bridal language in these passages? There is bridal language woven throughout the whole Bible, but we haven't learned how to hear it. When I married my husband, John, my name was no longer Turner. It became Valencia. He gave me his name. I've been telling you that you have the name of Jesus, and you are now Mrs. Jesus Christ. Do you see it? He's given you His name. It's not like being given the name of Smith or Jones, not that those are bad names. But this name carries the authority of Heaven. There is no name higher than the name of Jesus. So, He not only gives you a bridal headpiece to wear, and new garments to wear, He also gives you a new name. Even though I am a Valencia now on this Earth, I carry the mantle and authority of my King Jesus. I carry His name wherever I go.

Let's look more closely at Isaiah 62:4. "You shall no longer be termed [called] Forsaken...." What does the word *forsaken* mean? Rejected, abandoned, betrayed. God said, you won't be called Forsaken any longer. What will you be called? Hephzibah! *Hephzibah* means "My delight is in her." That's what God calls you: "I am delighted in you!" You can't go around saying, "I feel like God is mad at me. I think God is upset with me." No! Your name is *Hephzibah*. His delight is in you. And your land shall be called *Beulah*, which means *married*.

Do you remember that old song "Beulah Land?" What it meant was "Married Land." We've been singing that song for decades without knowing what it means. Listen, if you're single, and you want to be married, start confessing this scripture over yourself. Call yourself Hephzibah, and prophesy over your life that you live in Beulah land. Declare what God says over you.

Isaiah 62:5 goes on to say, "Just as the bridegroom rejoices over the bride, So shall your God rejoice over you..." He says He *delights* in you and He *rejoices* over you. There's a scripture that says, "He surrounds us with songs of deliverance" and He sings love songs over us. That's difficult for our natural, carnal mind to understand. We've been programmed wrong. We find it hard to believe that God in Heaven would sing love songs over us. You know, sometimes when you're beating yourself up and listening to the devil's condemnation, just take a moment and say, "Hold on. God calls me Hephzibah. He delights in me. He's not mad at me. He loves me!" Speak God's Word over yourself!

Let's look at Hosea chapter 2 once again. We've looked at it before but haven't fully gleaned all that is contained in this passage. You might recall that Hosea 2 talks about how God "allured His Bride into the wilderness."

Hosea 2:14-15 (NKJV)
14 "Therefore, behold, I will allure her, will bring her into the wilderness, and speak comfort to her.
15 I will give her her vineyards from there, and the Valley of Achor [Valley of Trouble] *as a door of hope; she shall sing there, as in the days of her youth, as in the day when she came up from the land of Egypt.*

That's when you got saved. God is saying, "I'm going to restore her back to that first love... to the joy of her salvation." When you come up out of the wilderness you're going to have a deeper love affair with your King than you've ever had before. And, from that place you're going to start singing like when you first came out of Egypt... when you first got saved.

Hosea 2:16 (NKJV)
"And it shall be, in that day," says the Lord, "That you will call Me 'My Husband,' and no longer call Me 'My Master,'

Now, here's what I wanted to get to. It's found in Hosea 2:19-20. This is the part we haven't gone over completely yet. Watch this:

Hosea 2:19-20 (NKJV)
19 "I will betroth you to Me forever; yes, I will betroth you to Me in righteousness and justice, in lovingkindness and mercy;
20 I will betroth you to Me in faithfulness, and you shall know the Lord.

Did you catch that? "And you shall know the Lord." You really, truly don't *know* Him until you know Him as your Husband. You truly don't know Him until you know that He calls you His Beloved. He desires you, He delights in you, and He is in love with you. I know for men, this is probably a difficult thing to say, "He desires me. He delights in me." The macho side of a man may keep him from saying these words, but we're not talking *flesh*... we're talking *Spirit*. You've got to remember that in Christ "there is neither male nor female." We are Spirit beings, created in His image, so we've got to think about this in spiritual terms. Don't get hung up in your human understanding of this. We are the Bride of Christ. We don't fully know Him until we know Him as our Husband.

BRIDAL LANGUAGE IN THE NEW TESTAMENT

Now, let's turn to the New Testament for more references to the bridal language found in the scriptures. First, let's look at the Gospels.

John 3:29 (NKJV)
He who has the bride is the bridegroom; but the friend of the bridegroom, who stands and hears him, rejoices greatly because of the bridegroom's voice....

These are the words of John the Baptist and he's referring to Jesus as the bridegroom. John is saying, "I'm just a friend of the bridegroom... Jesus is the bridegroom. The bride doesn't belong to me. She belongs to Him, and I'm happy for Him."

In Mark 2, Jesus was asked why His disciples didn't fast like the disciples of John the Baptist, and the disciples of the Pharisees. Jesus replied:

Mark 2:19-20 (NKJV)
19 "Can the friends of the bridegroom fast while the bridegroom is with them? As long as they have the bridegroom with them they cannot fast.
20 But the days will come when the bridegroom will be taken away from them, and then they will fast in those days.

This is another clear reference to Jesus being called the *bridegroom*.

Now, let's look at the letters of Paul to find other, clear references to bridal language.

2 Corinthians 11:2 (NIV)
I am jealous for you with a godly jealousy [speaking as Christ]. *I promised you* [betrothed you] *to one husband, to Christ, so that I might present you as a pure virgin to him.*

Did you catch that? "I *betrothed* you to one husband." We don't use the word *betrothed* anymore. Instead, we use the word *engaged*. *Betrothed* is bible language for *engaged*. But there are major differences between the Bible word *betrothed* and the modern word *engaged*.

Betrothal was a literal covenant and contract. It was much more binding than our modern-day engagement. As a matter of fact, if a couple who was betrothed to one another decided to end the relationship it had to be nullified through a legal divorce.

In another of Paul's letters to the churches we find this reference to bridal language in the book of Ephesians:

Ephesians 5:25-29, 32 (NKJV)
25 Husbands, love your wives, just as Christ also loved the church and gave Himself for her,
26 that He might sanctify and cleanse her with the washing of water by the word,
27 that He might present her to Himself a glorious church, not having spot or wrinkle or any such thing, but that she should be holy and without blemish.
28 So husbands ought to love their own wives as their own bodies; he who loves his wife loves himself.
29 For no one ever hated his own flesh, but nourishes and cherishes

it, just as the Lord does the church.
32 This is a great mystery, but I speak concerning Christ and the church [a husband loving his wife].

So, this is just two snippets of scripture from Paul's epistles that contain bridal language and reiterate that Christ is the Husband of the Church. Now, let's look at the book of Revelation.

Revelation 19:7 (NKJV)
... the marriage of the Lamb has come, and His wife has made herself ready.

Now, look at Revelation 22:17. What does it say? Does it say, "The Spirit and the *Church* say, 'Come'"? No! What does it say?

Revelation 22:17 (NKJV)
And the Spirit and the bride say, "Come...."

He's not coming back for a Church. He's coming back for a Bride! Now, all of this was just an introduction to where I want to take you.

FROM THE BEGINNING TO THE END

Our identity at the end of the age is a Bride who is longing for the return of her Bridegroom. That is our end-time identity as a Church. We shouldn't have the old-fashioned church mindset of "Hold the fort until He comes back, and get as many into the ark as we can." No! We've got to take hold of our identity as the Bride He is returning for. It is a recurring theme from Genesis to Revelation. Jesus is the Alpha and Omega, the beginning and the end. So, it stands to reason that His purpose and plan for His people would be clearly seen from Genesis (the beginning) all the way through Revelation (the end).

The book of Genesis began with a wedding in the garden. After

God created man, He said, "It is not good for man to be alone." So God made a woman for man. He took a rib from man's side and fashioned it into Eve, the first woman. Adam said, "This is bone of my bone and flesh of my flesh." And the two became one. That was the first wedding, and it's right there at the beginning, in Genesis.

Then, at the very end of the Bible, in the book of Revelation, everything will culminate with a wedding. Everything will culminate with the marriage supper of the Lamb. Everything from the book of Genesis to the book of Revelation is pointing to this one event. It all began with a wedding and it's all going to end with a wedding. And, *you* are the Bride!

THE JEWISH WEDDING TRADITION

Now, Jewish tradition teaches that the joining of a man and woman in the covenant of marriage is actually a reenactment, or replica, of God's covenant and relationship with us. We really need to learn to think that way! John 12 and 13 records the Last Supper of Jesus with His disciples, on the night He was betrayed. He was getting ready to go to the cross. He knows where He's going, but the disciples still haven't gotten it yet. He tells them:

John 14:1-3 (NKJV)
1 Let not your heart be troubled; you believe in God, believe also in Me.
2 In My Father's house are many mansions; if it were not so, I would have told you. I go to prepare a place for you.
3 And if I go and prepare a place for you, I will come again and receive you to Myself; that where I am, there you may be also.

Now, what you might not have been aware of is that Jesus was speaking to them directly out of a Jewish marriage ceremony. There is part of the Jewish marriage ceremony where the groom will say to the bride, "I am going away to prepare a place for you, so that where I am you will be with me always." Jesus was speaking in bridal language to the disciples. He was speaking to them in terms taken from the customs of their time. He was speaking to them with the same words the bridegroom speaks to his betrothed.

THE BETROTHAL PROCESS

The Hebrew betrothal is defined by a period of sanctification and setting apart of an individual. This is important to understand, so I'll reiterate that thought. The betrothal period is a time of sanctification and setting apart. We, as the Church (the Bride of Christ) are in this season, this time of sanctification. Jesus is preparing a place for us, but we are also preparing ourselves for His return. The Bible says, "Come out from among them and be ye separate, says the Lord." Unless we understand the paradigm of the bride and the bridegroom, we won't understand the period of time that we are in as the Church. We wouldn't "play" with the world if we really understood that we are betrothed to the King forever, and are being prepared and set apart to be His Bride… a Bride who will rule and reign with the King forever.

The meaning behind the Jewish betrothal process has always been much greater than the meaning behind the engagement process of western culture. The Jewish betrothal was so binding that the couple would need a religious divorce called a *get* in order to annul the contract. People today get engaged and then break it off if things don't seem to be working out. Not so with the Jewish betrothal. It was definitely a more binding agreement than what we know in our culture today.

Deuteronomy 24:1-4 gives some of the details that must be followed when getting a divorce. It's important to note that the husband was the only one who could legally request an annulment. The bride had no say in the matter. Even if the bride didn't want to be betrothed or married anymore, it didn't matter. It was the husband's decision. The betrothal customs and the picture of marriage found in the Jewish traditions gives us a much clearer understanding of our relationship with Jesus. We have to come to a place where we see Him as our Bridegroom King!

Now, in America, (and in western culture) our marriage process goes something like this: 1) We see a significant other that we're attracted to. 2) We date. 3) We fall in love. 4) We become engaged and on an agreed upon date. 5) We go through a short ceremony where we exchange vows with one another. That's it! Now we're married! The process can be as long or as short as you want it to be. Some people like an hour-long ceremony, while others prefer a short, 5-minute ceremony. I prefer the longer ceremony myself, since it's a life-long covenant that's being made. To me, the ceremony should have more substance to it than what is typically found in a short, 5-minute ceremony.

But, in the ancient Jewish wedding, the process was very different from what we are used to. So, when God says, "I have betrothed you to Me forever," this isn't something we should take lightly. It's not like, "I got engaged last week, and I'm going to get married next month." It's not that trivial.

TWO STAGES

The Jewish wedding was performed in two stages.

The first stage was the betrothal stage, but the betrothal stage was just as important, and just as much a part of the wedding as the actual culmination and consummation of the marriage itself. In the betrothal stage, a promise to be married was agreed upon in a mutual contract. When we get engaged today, there's nothing legal about it. It's like getting a friendship ring. It's like saying, "We're going steady." No contracts are signed. But, when God instituted marriage, the betrothal portion of the marriage agreement was just as important as the marriage ceremony. It was legally binding.

The second stage was the consummation of the marriage. The consummation is when the marriage agreement is carried out to the furthest extent and degree of completion that is possible. It is when the two individuals literally become one in sexual union, in the same manner in which Adam *knew* Eve in the Garden of Eden.

THE BETROTHAL STAGE

The betrothal stage is the present stage that the church is in right now. We are in a betrothal stage. And, remember, the betrothal stage is a legally binding stage of the relationship. We are in a legal contract with the Bridegroom. We are officially married, it's just that the culmination of the wedding ceremony hasn't happened yet.

So, we must take our salvation that seriously. People get saved, then they backslide, then they get saved again and backslide again. It's just like being engaged one day and then breaking off the engagement the next day because you don't want to be committed to the other person. We are not *engaged* to Christ... we are *betrothed*. There's a difference! We are in a legal covenant with God.

AN ARRANGED MARRIAGE

One of the first things we need to keep in mind about the Jewish betrothal is that Jewish marriages were often arranged. Fathers chose the bride. Surely you catch the significance of that thought as it pertains to our betrothal to Christ! Let's look at a couple of verses that support this thought.

John 15:16 (NKJV)
You did not choose Me, but I chose you...

Ephesians 1:4 (NKJV)
just as He chose us in Him before the foundation of the world, that we should be holy and without blame before Him in love,.

You see, you thought this was your idea. You thought this was your decision to follow Christ. But, this was something *He chose*. He chose you. This relationship was pre-arranged by the Father!

OBTAINING A WIFE

That leads us to the second part of the betrothal process. The father and the son leave their home and travel to the girls' home for the purpose of obtaining a wife, and establishing a marriage covenant, called a *ketubah*. Similarly, Jesus left Heaven and came to Earth for the purpose of obtaining a bride and establishing a covenant with us.

NEGOTIATING THE BRIDAL PRICE

The third part of the betrothal process was the bridal price had to be established. The father, the son (bridegroom) and the father of the chosen girl would meet to negotiate the bridal price. The price that they agreed upon was a direct reflection of the value that the young man placed on her. He understood that he was going to have to pay dearly. The measure of love is how much the bridegroom gives. Jesus paid our bridal price. Jesus, our Bridegroom, paid the highest price for us... His very life.

1 Corinthians 6:20 (NKJV)
(For) you were bought at a price...

1 Peter 1:18-19 (NKJV)
18 knowing that you were not redeemed with corruptible things, like silver or gold, from your aimless conduct received by tradition from your fathers,
19 but with the precious blood of Christ, as of a lamb without blemish and without spot.

Jesus gave everything; He paid the highest price to purchase us as His Bride. This takes salvation to another level, beloved!

THE DATE IS SET

The fourth stage of the betrothal process was that the date was set by the father and the son. They return to their home and the son does whatever he has to do to get that bridal price, selling whatever he needs to sell. Now, Jesus told us that He gave all to purchase His Bride in Matthew 13:44.

Matthew 13:44 (NKJV)
Again, the kingdom of heaven is like treasure hidden in a field, which a man found and hid; and for joy over it he goes and sells all that he has and buys that field.

He was talking about marriage, and the disciples knew it. He was speaking to them in bridal language. This man found a treasure in a field and he wanted it so badly that he sold everything he owned to purchase it. Similarly, God saw you and me on this earth and He said, "This is such a great treasure, I'm going to give everything I own and value to purchase it." And that is exactly what He did.

RITUAL EMERSION

The next stage of the betrothal process was the ritual emersion called the *mikvah*. Usually, prior to the formal betrothal time, it was common for the bride and groom to be separately taken into a ritual emersion which was symbolic of spiritual cleansing. What do believers do after they receive salvation? They go through an emersion... it's called baptism. In baptism we are symbolically saying that we are separating from our former way of life into a new one. Ephesians 5:26-27 reminds us that God sanctifies and cleanses us by the washing of the water by the Word that He might present us to Himself as a glorious Church. He says, "I am washing you. I'm separating you from your old lifestyle and preparing you to be a Bride."

In the *mikvah*, the bride was to disrobe herself and dip down into the pool of water to signify that she is being cleansed and sanctified for her husband. When we go into the baptismal waters, not only are we separating ourselves from our old life, but we are coming into a marriage covenant with our King.

Hebrews 10:22 (NKJV)
Let us draw near with a true heart in full assurance of faith, having our hearts sprinkled from an evil conscience and our bodies washed with pure water.

There's a cleansing and sanctification that should take place in our lives after salvation, and our water baptism symbolizes that.

THE BETROTHAL DINNER

The sixth stage of the betrothal process is next... the betrothal dinner. The young man and his parents go to the girl's house for this betrothal dinner. This is done publicly under a *chuppah*, which is a canopy, and there they make a public declaration of their intentions of being betrothed, not married. This isn't the wedding ceremony. This is still part of the betrothal process. As they publicly declare their intentions, a cup is directly in front of the two of them.

A PUBLIC DECLARATION

Matthew 10:32 (NKJV)
Therefore whoever confesses Me before men, him I will also confess before My Father who is in heaven.

There is a public confession that He is calling us to make. He wants us to declare publicly our intentions to be His Bride. We often tell new converts at our church, "Tell other people that you've accepted Jesus as Lord. Make a public confession." This is something that was done way back in the Old and New Testament.

THE TERMS OF THE MARRIAGE COVENANT

So during this part of the betrothal process, during the public declarations, while the cup is still in front of them, they present the marriage covenant. The terms of the agreement are declared. There, in public with everybody witnessing this, after the terms are read and agreed upon, the cup was drunk by both the bridegroom and the bride, signifying that the agreement is solidified. Now, think back to the Last Supper. Jesus is with His disciples and says:

Luke 22:20 (NIV)
This cup is the new covenant in my blood, which is poured out for you.

Jesus was presenting the price of the covenant, and the disciples understood because they knew bridal language. They knew what He was saying.

Matthew 26:26-28 (NIV)
26 While they were eating, Jesus took bread, and when he had given thanks, he broke it and gave it to his disciples, saying, "Take and eat; this is my body."
27 Then he took a cup, and when he had given thanks, he gave it to them, saying, "Drink from it, all of you.
28 This is my blood of the covenant, which is poured out for many for the forgiveness of sins.

He is saying, "I want you to take this marriage contract. When you drink from this cup you are taking part in a covenant with Me." This should change the way you look at the communion table!

The *ketubah* was a legal document. It could only be broken by divorce. The document outlined the price of the bride, the terms of the agreement, and the promise to take care of the bride. The way the bride showed that she accepted the terms of the *ketubah* was by drinking from the cup that was in front of them during the public ceremony.

The New Testament is our covenant. Jesus said, "This is the new covenant." Everything changed at the point when Jesus and the disciples drank from the cup together. A covenant was agreed upon and ratified, even though the disciples didn't fully understand all that was being established in that moment. The old was passing away and the new had come. Where we once called him "Master," we now call Him, "My Husband."

It's a love affair. It's a marriage. Every time we partake of communion, we shouldn't just "do this in remembrance of Me." When we drink from that cup we're saying, "I accept the contract. I receive the covenant. I receive the betrothal. I will be your wife forever. I am betrothed to you forever." I'm no longer just partaking of Holy Communion. Now I'm having a covenant with my Bridegroom. His part of the covenant is stated in Ephesians 5:25-27. He promises to love you. He promises to give Himself up for you. He promises to sanctify you and cleanse you, so He can present you as a glorious Bride. In Hebrews 13:5, He further promises, "I will never leave you or forsake you." That's bridal language. He's saying, "I will never divorce you or abandon you."

DRINKING FROM THE CUP

In the next stage of the betrothal process, the father asks if the girl will accept the proposal... will she accept the covenant... will she accept the contract. If she agrees, she will drink from the cup. When the girl accepts the covenant, she then enters into the father's house to meet with the father and son. It's important to remember that this is just the first stage of the marriage... this is just the betrothal. When you accept Christ, that is the first step of entering into the covenant. At salvation, you enter into the betrothal stage. You just accepted the terms of the covenant.

Next, the father offers the cup to the groom. The young man drinks and says, "I'm willing to pay the price in order to make her my wife." Jesus drank from the cup in the Garden of Gethsemane.

Matthew 26:39 (NIV)
Going a little farther, he fell with his face to the ground and prayed, "My Father, if it is possible, may this cup be taken from me. Yet not as I will, but as you will."

He knew He had to drink of the cup to purchase the Bride. Wow!

The next thing that happens after the groom says, "I accept the price," is that the bride drinks from the cup. This signifies her willingness to enter into the marriage. She's saying, "I accept your gift and your life, and I offer you my life in return."

Matthew 26:27-28 (NIV)
27 Then he took a cup, and when he had given thanks, he gave it to them, saying, "Drink from it, all of you.
28 This is my blood of the covenant, which is poured out for many for the forgiveness of sins.

You see, this is part of the contract. Once the groom and bride drank from the cup, the young man would hand over the bridal price to the father. Jesus handed over the bridal price in Luke 23:46 when He said, "Father, into your hands I commit my Spirit."

Jesus' blood was the purchase price that He paid so we could become His Bride.

GIFTS GIVEN AS A PLEDGE

The next thing that happened was that gifts were presented to the bride-to-be. The word that was used for the gifts that were given was the Greek word *charismata*. These gifts were the *pledge* and the *seal* (or the promise) that he would return for her. Jesus gave us gifts when He went to Heaven. Let's look at Ephesians 1:13-14.

Ephesians 1:13-14 (NASB)
13 ... you were sealed in Him with the Holy Spirit of promise,
14 who is given as a pledge of our inheritance, with a view to the redemption of God's own possession....

The promised Holy Spirit is a gift guaranteeing that He will be back for us. "You were sealed with the Holy Spirit of promise." That was the seal of the marriage covenant.

THE VEIL OF SANCTIFICATION

The gifts were proof to the bride that the marriage contract was sealed. When she saw the gifts, she knew he was serious. The gifts sealed the deal. Once the bridegroom gives something of value to the bride, the betrothal process is completed. At that point, the bride puts a veil over her face signifying that she is now betrothed. She is saying, "I am now set apart for this man. I will have no other lovers but Him." The actual ceremony of putting the veil over her face is called the *Kiddushin*, which means *sanctification*.

1 Corinthians 1:2 (NKJV)
To the church of God which is at Corinth, to those who are sanctified in Christ Jesus....

1 Corinthians 6:11 (NKJV)
And such were some of you. But you were washed, but you were sanctified, but you were justified in the name of the Lord Jesus....

Hebrews 10:10 tells us that we have been sanctified by this covenant. What a new meaning and understanding we can now have of the word *sanctification*. Now, the bride promises to pay a dowry. This is her part in the contract agreement. 1 Corinthians 6 tells us the payment of our dowry is a yielded life – a life that is set apart. We promise that we will not give our heart to any other lover. That bridal veil over the bride's face signified that she was set apart for her husband; that she belonged only to him. No one else was allowed to look upon her because she was considered a married woman, even though the marriage hasn't been consummated. They hadn't taken the final vows to one another yet, but that veil said that she was going to walk in purity, reserving herself for him only.

Romans 12:1 (NKJV)
I beseech you therefore, brethren, by the mercies of God, that you present your bodies a living sacrifice, holy, acceptable to God, which is your reasonable service.

1 Corinthians 6:17 (NKJV)
But he who is joined to the Lord is one spirit with Him.

PREPARING A PLACE

The next thing that happens is the bridegroom goes and prepares a bridal chamber. I opened this chapter with John 14, "I go to prepare a place for you." Jesus was speaking in bridal language. So, right after the bride puts the veil over her face, setting herself apart for her bridegroom, the bridegroom goes to prepare a place for her. He (Jesus) made a promise that He'd be back when it is ready.

John 14:2-3 (NKJV)
2 In My Father's house are many mansions; if it were not so, I would have told you. I go to prepare a place for you.
3 And if I go and prepare a place for you, I will come again and receive you to Myself; that where I am, there you may be also.

The disciples completely understood at that time that Jesus was speaking bridal language. They'd seen many weddings. Some of them were married. They knew the marriage rituals of their day. They knew when a woman put a veil over her face that she was being set apart for the bridegroom. They knew that the bridegroom had an obligation to go and prepare a place for his bride. They knew about the marriage contract – the *Ketubah*.

A NAME CHANGE

Once the bridegroom leaves to go and prepare a place for the bride, she is henceforth referred to as "the one who is bought with a price." She says, "I am Hephzibah and I was bought with a price." The veil on her face reminds her that she is betrothed to her bridegroom and her affections are for him only. No other men, no other lovers, will look upon her face. She takes on his name at this point, and is considered his wife legally. She has all the legal privileges associated with his name, even though the marriage has not yet been fully consummated.

Mark 16:17 (NKJV)
And these signs will follow those who believe: In my name they will....

The Bride of Christ has been given the legal privilege of using Jesus' name. He said they'd cast out demons in His name, and speak in new tongues in His name. They will lay hands on the sick in His name, and they will recover.

Acts 11:26 (NKJV)
.... And the disciples were first called Christians in Antioch.

Christian means *representing Christ*. Believers are named with the name of Christ. We are called the Bride of Christ. We have taken on a new name because we are betrothed to Jesus. My name is *Hephzibah*.... His delight is in me. My land is called *Beulah*... I am married. I have no other gods before me. I have no other lovers. I have a veil of separation over me. His Spirit has sealed me. He has given gifts to me. He has guaranteed that He will come back for me.

THE BRIDAL CHAMBER

Now, when the bridegroom hands the bride the marriage covenant, at that point he returns to his father's house and begins building. He begins building onto the father's house. Basically, he's building an addition to his father's house.

Rabbis would be consulted in this step. They would be called upon to confirm that the new bridal chamber being prepared for the bride is better than the house and chamber where the bride currently lived. Listen, where you're going will be far better than what you're living in right now.

Only the father could judge when the new bridal chamber was completed. And, when the young man could go and claim his bride was determined by the father, as well. The son had no idea when he would be sent by the father to get his bride.

Matthew 25:13 (NKJV)
Watch therefore, for you know neither the day nor the hour in which the Son of Man is coming.

Matthew 24:36 (NIV)
But about that day or hour no one knows, not even the angels in heaven, nor the Son, but only the Father alone.

PREPARATION TIME

As the young man was preparing the bridal chamber, the bride was preparing her wedding garment. Her time waiting on the bridegroom was not a time of idleness. It was a time of preparation. Jesus is coming back, not for a church, but for a glorious Bride... someone who is clothed properly... someone who knows who she is and what she carries, and what she wears.

Revelation 19:7-8 (NIV)
7 Let us rejoice and be glad and give him glory! For the wedding of the Lamb has come, and his bride has made herself ready.
8 Fine linen, bright and clean, was given her to wear. (Fine linen stands for the righteous acts of God's holy people.)

Isaiah 61:10 (NKJV)
I will greatly rejoice in the Lord, My soul shall be joyful in my God; For He has clothed me with the garments of salvation, He has covered me with the robe of righteousness, as a bridegroom decks himself with ornaments, and as a bride adorns herself with her jewels.

BRIDAL GARMENTS

Now, as we opened this chapter, we read from Isaiah 61:3 and mentioned the "garments of praise." Praise is part of your garments as the Bride of Christ. Praise says, "I love my King. I'm in love with Him. I worship Him." We saw where the Lord gives us a "garland instead of ashes" and that garland is actually a bridal headpiece that He's given us to wear. Proverbs 31:25 says, "She is clothed with strength and dignity." So we see that praise, strength and dignity are all mentioned as clothing. The wedding garments are not literal, physical clothes. These are spiritual garments that we are robed in.

ARE YOUR LAMPS FILLED WITH OIL?

One of the ways the bride got herself ready for the bridegroom's return is by making sure she had extra oil in her lamp. That is because many times the father would send his son for his bride in the middle of the night, unexpectedly. The bride had to be prepared for a nighttime arrival. It was common for the bridegroom to return in secret, suddenly and unannounced, and often times in the middle of the night. Matthew 25:1-13 is the parable of the ten virgins. Five were wise. They were watching and ready with their oil lamps filled. The other five were foolish and were not prepared. At midnight a cry was heard, "Behold, the bridegroom is coming, go out to meet him." The ten virgins were awakened... out of their sleep. You need to catch the significance of that because many who are in the church are asleep today.

The five foolish virgins were not ready. They had no oil in their lamps. They were not watching and waiting for the bridegroom's return. They were not clothed. They were not dressed. They were not set apart. There was no veil over their faces.

The season of waiting is coming to an end. The Bride should be telling everyone she knows that her Bridegroom is coming soon. She should be saying, "He loves me. He gave me a covenant. He gave me gifts and a promise of His return. We drank from the cup together. We've made a covenant together!"

In Song of Solomon 6:3, the Shulamite woman says, "I am my beloved's and he is mine." But when you go further to Song of Solomon 7:10, she says, "I am my beloved's, and his desire is toward me." She's calling herself "Hephzibah," *His desire is for me.* She went from being this little woman who felt dark and afraid, to "Now he desires me." That's the results of evangelism right there. Jesus said, in Mark 16:15, "Go into all the world and preach the gospel." Tell them about your King. Tell them about how you are betrothed to Him forever. The world needs to hear about this marriage relationship between Jesus and His Bride.

If she grows weary in waiting for her King's return, she need only remember the covenant price He paid for her. She rereads the marriage covenant. She rereads the contract He left with her... the word of God. If someone else offers her another contract she refuses it, because she belongs to Him. "A stranger's voice she will not hear."

The Jewish Wedding Ceremony

RENEW YOUR VOWS

Let's read about The Lord's Supper from 1 Corinthians 11.

1 Corinthians 11:24 (NKJV)
24 and when He had given thanks, He broke it and said, "Take, eat; this is My body which is broken for you; do this in remembrance of Me."

He's saying here, "This is the marriage price I am paying to obtain you as my Bride." When He says, "do this in remembrance of Me," this is like a renewal of your wedding vows. Some couples renew their wedding vows on their 25th and 50th anniversary. Every time we remember what He did for us, as we partake of the communion elements, it is just like we are renewing our vows to Him.

1 Corinthians 11:25 (NKJV)
25 In the same manner He also took the cup after supper, saying, "This cup is the new covenant in My blood. This do, as often as you drink it, in remembrance of Me."

"In remembrance of Me." Communion is not just a time to remember what the Lord did for us through His crucifixion. In regards to the covenant cup in the betrothal process, it is a time to remember the terms of the covenant agreement. It is a time to remember He has promised to return after He's finished preparing a place for us in the Father's House. Knowing what you now know about the Jewish marriage custom, you should never take communion in the same way again.

As the time draws near for the bridegroom's return, the bride must gather her bridesmaids together. These are the daughters of Jerusalem. These are the onlookers in our lives... our friends, family and acquaintances. They must be prepared for his return, just as much as the bride. We must let them know our bridegroom is returning. We must help them get prepared for the event.

GET PREPARED!

Often times the bride would actually sleep in her wedding dress because she didn't know when the bridegroom would be coming.

1 Thessalonians 5:2 (NIV)
For you know very well that the day of the Lord will come like a thief in the night.

She gathers her bridesmaids; those are the virgins with the oil lamps. Those are the daughters of Jerusalem. Now everything is ready.

The father inspects the bridal suite, making sure everything is ready. Meanwhile, the bridegroom is waiting on his father. He's hoping his bride is ready and waiting. He doesn't know when his father will give the final word. Then the father says, "Now! Now's the time." Upon hearing the father's word, the friend of the bridegroom would run on ahead of the wedding procession to announce to the bride, "Behold, the bridegroom is coming!"

At that point, a shofar (trumpet) was blown. That gave her just enough time to light her lamp and get out of bed.

1 Corinthians 15:52 (NKJV)
In a moment, in the twinkling of an eye, at the last trumpet. For the trumpet will sound, and the dead will be raised incorruptible, and we shall be changed.

She looks like a bride now, all lit up, ready and waiting. And the groom would charge in and take her away to his father's house. And then there would be a seven-day celebration. In Matthew 25:10, when the bridegroom came and took the bride to his father's house, the five foolish virgins went to buy more oil for their lamps, because they had run out of oil. Only those who were ready and waiting went in with him into the father's house for the celebration. The doors were shut behind them. Those who were not ready, like the five foolish virgins, were left outside. They did not get to be a part of the marriage celebration.

This is the culmination of the marriage. Everything has led to this moment in time. Now the bridegroom and bride are united in marriage.

IT IS FINISHED!

The Hebrew word for *bride* is *Kallah*. It means "to finish, to complete, to make perfect." When Jesus hung on the cross and took His last breath and said, "It is finished," that word *finished* is *Kallah*. So, He said, "I have purchased the Bride. It is a marriage! It is completed! I did it, Father. I paid the bridal price! I purchased her, God! I drank the cup and did what you sent me to do. She's now mine!" And what God has joined together let no man put asunder, Amen!

CLOSING REMARKS

Ephesians 3:16-19 (NKJV)
"That He would grant you, according to the riches of His glory, to be strengthened with might through His Spirit in the inner man, that Christ may dwell in your hearts through faith; that you, being rooted and grounded in love, may be able to comprehend with all the saints, what is the width and length and depth and height – to know the love of Christ which passes knowledge; that you may be filled with all the fullness of God."

It is my desire for those who read *The Emerging Warrior Bride* that the pages of this book will begin to awaken your spirit, heal your emotions and ignite a passion in you for your King, as you begin to comprehend experientially His love for you.

It is my earnest prayer that upon your reading of this book, that you will be brought into a new and deeper place in your love for Him. As you continue to rise up in this hour as the end-time Bride of Christ, let Him continue to kiss you with the revelation of His love for you. Allow it to transform every area of your life.

Song of Solomon 8:5
"Who is this coming up from the wilderness, leaning on her beloved?"

It is the Bride of Christ and you are a part of this company. She is rising up out of her wilderness, clothed in new strength, leaning on her beloved. Together, they are going forth, arm in arm, side by side, into the vineyards.

It is time to wear your wedding ring confidently. He is your beloved!

Ephesians 3:20-21 (NKJV)
"Now to Him who is able to do exceedingly abundantly above all that we ask or think, according to the power that works in us, to Him be glory in the church by Christ Jesus to all generations forever and ever. Amen."

Judith Valencia